Noah Webster

Twayne's United States Authors Series

Lewis Leary, Editor
University of North Carolina, Chapel Hill

TUSAS 465

NOAH WEBSTER, JUN. ESQ.

This portrait of Webster appeared in many editions of
his schoolbooks. From *An American Selection . . . (1794)*.
Courtesy of the Colby College Library.

Noah Webster

By Richard J. Moss

Colby College

Twayne Publishers • *Boston*

Noah Webster

Richard J. Moss

Copyright © 1984 by G. K. Hall & Company
All Rights Reserved
Published by Twayne Publishers
A Division of G. K. Hall & Company
70 Lincoln Street
Boston, Massachusetts 02111

Book Production by John Amburg

Book Design by Barbara Anderson

Printed on permanent/durable acid-free
paper and bound in the United States of America.

Library of Congress Cataloging in Publication Data

Moss, Richard J.
    Noah Webster.

    (Twayne's United States authors series; TUSAS 465)
    Bibliography: p. 122
    Includes index.
    1. Webster, Noah, 1758–1843. I. Title. II. Series.
PE64.W5M68   1984   423'.092'4 [B]   83-18558
ISBN 0-8057-7406-8

Contents

About the Author

Richard Moss was born and raised in Michigan. He received his doctorate in American History from Michigan State University in 1974. In the course of his career as an historian he has taught at Michigan State, Spring Arbor College, Carthage College, and the University of Wisconsin/Parkside. He also served for almost two years as an historical editor with the Michigan History Division. Presently, he is an associate professor of history at Colby College in Maine where he teaches courses in American cultural history and the colonial and early national periods. Mr. Moss has written articles on the press in the Federalist period, the historiography of the Jacksonian period, and a history of Detroit's Tiger Stadium.

Preface

Noah Webster must surely fall into that category of great men whose reputation rests on one great deed. Americans today habitually equate "Webster" with "dictionary" even if they are not sure whether the first name was Daniel or Noah; yet few realize that Noah Webster published the dictionary when he was seventy and that a long and fruitful life preceded its publication. Before turning to the study of language and the making of dictionaries Webster worked as a schoolteacher, a lawyer, and a newspaper editor. Writing incessantly, he turned out schoolbooks, political essays, essays on language, moralistic tracts, and scientific treatises. He wrote so much that a bibliography of his works runs to well over six hundred pages. His writings have been read by millions; his spelling book, for example, may well be the best-selling secular book in American history. Certainly influential, it shaped the young minds of millions of Americans who encountered it, often as their first schoolbook, in the nation's schools in the nineteenth century.

So, however trite it may seem, Webster was a man of many parts—complex, full of intellectual tensions and paradoxes. He lived (1758–1843) during a period in which America and the world experienced great changes; the American and French Revolutions were only the political expressions of the momentous transformations that occurred between 1758 and 1843. It is in his response to these political, social, religious, and economic changes that we discover Webster's importance. He encountered the full force of democratization and secularization as it gradually modernized American life, and he responded by growing more anxious and conservative in an attempt to establish for himself and his nation stable boundaries to an expanding and changing world. In no way did he entirely capitulate to either the past or future; instead, he kept one foot solidly planted in the unchanging rural Protestant Connecticut of his childhood, and with the other foot he tentatively explored the enlightened, secular, and democratic world of post-revolutionary America. The result was a life of tension and paradox, a life constructed of often conflicting and unblendable elements.

Thus, the Webster who appears in this study, generally retreated in the face of enlightened ideas, democracy, and secularism and embraced the notions inherited from his Puritan ancestors. Yet he was never fully a nineteenth-century Puritan; the radicalism of a revolutionary age had important and long-lasting effects on him. He groped his way through an age of great political and intellectual upheaval; the Webster who emerged was a paradoxical and perplexing blend of the old and the new.

I should say a word about the organization of this book. After an opening biographical sketch, it employs a topical approach. The reader will find chapters on Webster's schoolbooks and educational theory, his political thought, his labors as a journalist, and, finally, his work on language. These chapters, however, also follow a rough chronological line. Writing school texts was Webster's first major foray as an author; this gave way to politics, which in turn made way for journalism. After retiring from newspaper work, he devoted most of his later years to dictionaries and language. Yet he never entirely gave up any of his interests, and as he moved from one stage of his career to another, he carried along remnants of what had gone before.

The chapters that follow deal with a selection of Webster's major works. Webster wrote almost continuously for more than sixty years, and any exhaustive analysis of his writings would require a book four times the size of this one. In selecting books and essays from the body of Webster's work I have tried to present works that either had a significant impact on American thought, or ones that seem to most clearly represent important elements and transformations in Webster's thought. Finally, in most cases I have tried to let the works speak for themselves, but Webster was fond of explaining and expanding on his work in letters to friends and associates, and these letters appear occasionally as aides to understanding what Webster was up to.

Richard J. Moss

Colby College

Acknowledgments

A large number of people have been very helpful to me while I was writing this book. Hal Raymond, Charles Bassett, Joel Bernard, Jane Hunter, and Sam Atmore, all of Colby College, have helped, in one way or the other, to make this a better book. Their patience and skill have helped me eliminate errors and improve the text, but the final product, of course, remains my responsibility. Two very nonacademic friends, Sunny and Spike, have provided emotional support at every point along the way. Julie Cannon and Paige Tyson typed various drafts of the manuscript with skill and speed. The staff of the Colby College Library has been unfailingly patient and helpful.

While working on this book I have had the good fortune to teach at Colby College. The College has provided an excellent environment in which to teach and write. It also provided a research grant that allowed me to travel to New York and New Haven to work at the New York Public Library and in Yale's fine system of libraries. My wife, Jane, has served as Webster's ghost, always ready with advice on grammar and a lecture on the virtue of hard work and steady habits. Finally, I would like this book to be a small tribute to my late father for all I owe him.

Chronology

1812   Fall. Moved to Amherst, Massachusetts.

1822   Summer. Moved to New Haven.

1824–1825   Research trip to Europe.

1825   January. Completed unabridged dictionary in Cambridge, England.

1828   November. Published unabridged dictionary.

1832   August. *History of the United States.*

1833   September. Published revised edition of Bible.

1841   March. Published second edition of unabridged dictionary.

1843   May. *Collection of Papers.* Died in New Haven, 28 May.

Chapter One
An American Life

On Thanksgiving Day 1789, Noah Webster took his new bride home to meet his parents. Because his wife, Rebecca, was from a wealthy and prominent Boston family, her sophistication seemed painfully out of place at the elder Websters' simple West Hartford farm. Noah's nieces and nephews flocked around their new aunt marveling at her luxurious green brocade dress flowered with pink and red roses. The elegant and refined Boston lady seemed exotic in the plain Yankee home. The next day, however, Rebecca was back on more familiar ground entertaining in their new Hartford home "a large company of the most respectable citizens. . . ." She listed them in a letter to her brother; the Chief Justice of Connecticut Jesse Root, the author John Trumbull, and the State Treasurer Peter Colt headed a list of prominent and powerful members of Connecticut's elite. Two days or two dinners do not make a life, but in this case they graphically illustrated a fundamental aspect of the man who made America's great dictionary. He was an exemplar of a familiar American story: a simple farm boy trying to make it in the world of the rich and influential. Webster pushed and struggled to gain the approval and acceptance of those he deemed the elite, always with the thought that some day he would be counted as one of their number. Unfortunately for Webster, that elite and their world were in flux; even in conservative Connecticut, Webster lived to see the Standing Order disrupted and changed. The farm boy aimed at an elusive target, one that he never was able to hit squarely. In response he often returned in spirit to the solid values and virtues of his father's farm in the placid Connecticut countryside. Indeed, the conflict between the urban complexities and sophistication of Boston, Philadelphia, New York, Paris, and London and Webster's idealized rural New England boyhood was a central element in his life.[1]

Born 16 October 1758, Noah Webster inherited a full measure of Connecticut, Protestant pioneer heritage. From both sides of his family, young Noah heard stories of relatives, long dead, who had settled Connecticut and Massachusetts. On his father's side was John Web-

ster who had helped Thomas Hooker establish a Puritan colony at
Hartford. Noah's mother, Mercy Steele, could trace her family back
to Governor William Bradford of the Plymouth Colony. Noah's parents, however, were hardly prominent. They struggled to gain a living from a ninety-acre farm near Hartford where Noah Jr. was born
and where as a child he shared the daily farm chores with three brothers and a sister. Very little is known about Webster's childhood, but
we can guess that he worked hard and learned that honest labor and
thrift were virtues and that luxury and dissipation were not. He was
not, however, exposed to Christianity in its most rigorous Puritan
form; the family church, the Fourth Church of Hartford, was not
known for its piety. Still Webster always referred to his childhood as
religious and once suggested that it was not until his college years
that he fell "into vicious company . . . and contracted a habit of using profane language."[2]

Young Webster had an inclination toward study and books, not for
life on the farm. His father opposed this, but he finally relented and
sent the boy to study with Reverend Nathan Perkins, who provided
the training that allowed Webster eventually to enter Yale College.
Perkins was professional at his task; by the time of his death in 1839
he had prepared more than one hundred and fifty boys for college. At
the same time, Noah needed more than training to attend Yale; he
needed money. The funds came from his father who mortgaged the
family farm. This reflected a reality of New England life in the late
eighteenth century. Because of the great pressure to divide land, fathers such as Noah Sr. who owned only ninety acres to apportion
among his sons, were forced to find alternatives, such as college training, for some of them.[3]

College Years

Webster's years at Yale (1774–1778) were eventful and crucial to
his intellectual development. First of all, he acquired the skills that
served as the basis for his later studies in language. He also encountered a worldview that took him far from the fields of Connecticut.
He attended Yale at a time when religious fervor was declining and
secular interests were paramount. For example, the percentage of Yale
graduates entering the ministry had steadily declined for three decades. In the class of 1748 about half had become clergymen. In
Webster's 1778 class only ten percent did so.[4] Protest and revolution
were the order of the day, and Noah was often directly involved. In

1777 he and approximately twenty-five others walked out of chapel to protest the punishment of two of their classmates. Later, they had to publicly condemn themselves for their behavior. The class of 1778 was involved in one of America's first draft protests. When the Continental Army attempted to draft them, they saw it as a government intrusion on their rights. The class banded together, thought about hiring a lawyer, and taking the case to court. No record of the outcome exists.

The Revolution, however, was generally popular among Yale students. While they fought the draft, they did form a company that drilled on the green with the New Haven militia. In June 1775 Washington and his men passed through New Haven on their way to Cambridge. The militia escorted them, and as Webster put it, "it fell to my humble lot to lead this company in music."[5] He played the flute. The Revolution also caused severe disruptions at Yale. In December 1776 the students were dismissed because the college was unable to feed them. They returned in January but were sent home again in March.

During his college years Webster volunteered to join a small band of men who marched off to fight at Saratoga. Mostly from West Hartford, this unit was also very much a family affair since it was led by his father and included two of his brothers, Abraham and Charles. The march into New York came to nothing, however, since the unit arrived too late to participate in the battle. In the years after his graduation Webster referred to this episode as his revolutionary experience, often exaggerating the suffering he endured.

Webster's class of 1778 at Yale was a distinguished one. Many of his classmates went on to important positions: Josiah Meigs became president of the University of Georgia; Oliver Wolcott, Jr., served as Secretary of the Treasury; Uriah Tracy was a senator from Connecticut. Some of Webster's other classmates included the poet Joel Barlow, Abraham Bishop, who later became a prominent Jeffersonian politician in Connecticut, and Zephaniah Swift, the chief justice of the Connecticut Supreme Court.

The class of 1778 was one of the first to experience the liberalizing influence of Enlightenment and revolutionary thought. Timothy Dwight, the tutor to the class of 1777, was a major influence at Yale during this period. He replaced some of the ancient language study with English composition and literature. Ezra Stiles became president of the college in 1778, replacing the more conservative Naphtali

Daggett. Webster reflected this changing spirit in a senior oration called "A Short View of the Origin and Progress of the Science of Natural Philosophy." The hero of the piece was Newton, and Noah confessed that Natural Philosophy was his favorite intellectual pursuit. Webster's years at Yale were often disrupted by war and even by disease (typhoid epidemic), but Yale was beginning to reflect the sense of experimentalism and revolutionary ardor spawned by the conflict with Britain. Timothy Dwight's 1776 valedictory address, for example, suggested that Yale students would confront a world full of possibilities and awesome responsibilities:

You should by no means consider yourselves as members of a small neighbor, town or colony only, but as being concerned in laying the foundations of American greatness. Your wishes, your designs, your labors, are not to be confined by the narrow bounds of the present age, but are to comprehend succeeding generations, and pointed to immortality. . . . Remember that you are to act for the empire of America, and for a long succession of ages.[6]

Webster's difficult and egocentric personality apparently surfaced during his college years. His tutor, Joseph Buckminster, advised him to be less aggressive and more modest because "such is the perverseness of human nature they will be disposed to ridicule you and perhaps set you down among those who have too high an opinion of their importance."[7] This advice did little good; for the rest of his life Webster was repeatedly characterized as egocentric, vain, and too fond of self-promotion. In large part the charges were true; Webster tirelessly pushed himself and his works on those he believed could help him.

Schoolmaster and Schoolbooks

Graduation from Yale threw young Noah into a classic dilemma. After four years of college training, he was unsuited for most occupations open to him in revolutionary America. He had no clear calling; his only option was to return to his father's farm, but this route posed problems because the other children resented his college education. Soon it became clear that he must leave, for, as one historian put it, "demographic reality prevented him from remaining there." His father quite rudely pushed him from the nest. He handed Noah eight dollars in inflated Continental currency and said, "You must now seek your living; I can do no more for you." Young Noah fell into a depression and remained in his room for three days pondering his future. He never repaid his father for his college expenses and the elder Webster was forced to sell the farm in 1790.[8]

Noah did what so many in his position have done: he turned to schoolteaching. He first took a job at Glastonbury where he remained until the summer of 1779. Teaching was unpleasant and the pay so bad that he decided to try the legal profession. He was hired as an aide to Oliver Ellsworth, later chief justice of the United States Supreme Court, but soon Webster was back teaching, this time in Hartford. In 1780 he took a position as assistant to the registrar of deeds in Litchfield and returned to his legal studies. The next year he took the bar examination and failed along with all the others who took the test, but Noah promptly went back to Hartford, took the examination again, and passed. However, the law never provided him with a secure position in society. The Revolution had so disrupted American life that the legal profession was in a shambles. For a while he maintained an office in Hartford, but handled few cases and collected only small fees. He could neither repay his father nor make enough to live on.

Again he returned to teaching, but this time in his own school. In 1781 he moved to Sharon, Connecticut, and opened a school in a house owned by Governor John Cotton Smith. Webster taught the children of affluent refugees fleeing the revolutionary battles in New York, and he seemed to enjoy his position in Sharon, where he joined a small but thriving intellectual circle. His stay in Sharon was important for other reasons; he met the Huguenot, Reverend John Peter Tetard, with whom he studied French, German, Spanish, Latin, and history. As they read and discussed political philosophy, Webster seems to have sharpened his democratic tendencies. At Yale Webster had come to support universal white male suffrage and religious toleration; his relationship with Tetard extended and solidified these convictions.[9]

Webster also had his first serious romance while in Sharon. He was fond of female company, and his social life was full. At first he was drawn to Juliana Smith, but when that relationship failed, he fell in love with Rebecca Pardee. She was apparently fond of him as well, but she also had another suitor who was an officer in the Continental Army. When he returned, Webster found himself in a classic triangle. Soon Noah was rejected; Rebecca married the officer. Hurt and dejected, Webster closed his school and, in October 1781, left Sharon.

After his departure he wandered aimlessly through Connecticut. Failing to find employment, he eventually landed in Goshen, New York, virtually penniless. His life had reached its nadir, he was in a deep depression, and by his own account plagued by "gloomy forebodings." In desperate straits, he turned to teaching once more. This low point in Webster's life was also a turning point. Out of his failure and depression Webster emerged a strong propagandist for the Revolution, and he utilized his teaching experience to produce the first in a long series of schoolbooks that helped shape literally millions of young minds for more than a century. For a young man without ties and with little sense of direction the Revolution came to serve as an important structure in his life. Webster found in it, when he felt most like a failure, a meaning for life and threw himself tirelessly into the cause of an independent, utopian America. [10]

The most important and influential work by Webster during this period was Part I of *A Grammatical Institute of the English Language . . .* published in the fall of 1783. This was the famous spelling book; it was followed by Parts II and III, a grammar and a reader. Without doubt this work was motivated, in part, by revolutionary ardor, but it was also supposed to make money. Webster had found a cause, but he had not found economic security. He discovered to his dismay that the profits he might make from his schoolbooks were threatened by the lack of consistent copyright laws in the various states. His letter to the General Assembly of Connecticut in 1782 revealed his reasons for seeking a copyright:

Your memorialist [Webster], ever ambitious to promote the interest of literature and the honor and dignity of the American empire, designs the above mentioned work for the general benefit of youth in the United States. And in order to prevent spurious editions and to enable your memorialist to have the book under his correction, and especially to secure to him the pecuniary advantages of his own productions to which he conceives himself solely entitled, your memorialist therefore humbly prays that this honorable Assembly would . . . vest in your memorialist and assigns the exclusive right of printing, publishing and vending the said *American Instructor* in the State of Connecticut for and during the term of thirteen years. . . . [11]

For the rest of his life Noah Webster tirelessly battled for copyright laws that would protect American authors from having their creations pirated by unscrupulous printers. He sought to have the copyright term extended and to allow copyrights to pass on to the author's family. Without doubt Webster was the father of American copyright legislation, and for that American authors owe him a profound debt.

With the publication of Part I of his *Institute* and his agitation for copyright laws, Noah began to define himself not as a teacher or lawyer but as a writer who was to make his living manipulating words. It was not an easy transition to make; not until the early 1790s did he become fully disentangled from the schoolhouse and the courtroom. During the decade between 1782 and 1792 he slowly grew in stature as a national figure, his schoolbooks sold well, and his opinions on the crucial issues of the day reached a growing audience.

Yet during this decade he still sought, but never found, a steady source of income that would match his increasing stature as a national figure. In the spring of 1783 he returned to Hartford from Goshen and wrote almost continuously, finishing the second and third parts of his *Institute*. With their completion Webster had what amounted to a complete educational "system" to sell to the American public, yet still the money did not pour in. Webster was forced to spend time at the courthouse looking for law cases. While clients were few and far between, Noah kept busy. He roomed at the home of an old Yale friend, John Trumbull, and regularly turned up at Hartford social affairs with another Yale classmate and close friend, Joel Barlow. More important, he began to express himself on the issues of the day. He defended his recently published texts against the attacks of "Dilworth's Ghost." His books challenged the long dominance Thomas Dilworth's text had enjoyed in American classrooms. Webster returned the attack with equal fervor; he accused his unknown critic of being a frustrated printer with a pile of Dilworth's books to sell.

The Webster who used the newspapers to reply to the attacks of "Dilworth's Ghost" was a slightly arrogant and ambitious young man who understood that the controversy was good publicity for his schoolbooks. At times the debate seemed more like a farce. Dilworth, for example, challenged Webster to a duel and Webster responded that he doubted "single combat will ascertain the merits of the Institute." Much of the debate was devoted to petty bickering over grammatical niceties and the "Ghost's" allegations that Webster plagiarized much of the material in his schoolbooks. The "Ghost" portrayed Webster as proud and arrogant, and Webster replied that, indeed, he had "too much pride to stand indebted to Great Britain for books to learn our children the letters of the alphabet."[12] The whole controversy seemed like good fun to Webster, and when it eventually died down, his books were better known to his countrymen.

Webster also became involved in the controversy surrounding the Middletown Convention. During the Revolution the Continental Congress had passed a measure to prevent desertion by rebellious officers, granting them a bonus of half their current pay to be paid for life. After the war Congress altered the plan. Usually referred to as "Commutation," the National Congress agreed to pay the officers a lump sum equal to five years' full pay. The plan was very unpopular in Connecticut. In September 1783 a special convention, meeting at Middletown, asked the Connecticut Assembly to question the legality of the bonus and demanded that no state taxes go toward paying it. Anti-bonus forces helped push from office several important state officials including the governor, Jonathan Trumbull, who favored commutation. Webster wrote incessantly against the Convention and in favor of the bonus. He labeled the delegates at Middletown "Tories" and characterized special conventions as leading to anarchy. He was heartened in 1784 when the Middletown spirit declined and Connecticut passed a federal impost to fund the payment of the bonus. Yet this incident was important in Webster's life; it marked the first time his faith in the people was shaken. It was not the last: from the middle 1780s until his death, Noah grew less hopeful about the capacity of the people to participate in the political system. In November 1786 he wrote in the *Connecticut Courant* that

people in general are too ignorant to manage affairs that require great reading and an extensive knowledge of foreign nations. . . . For my own part, I confess, I was once as strong a republican as any man in America. *Now*, a republican is among the last kinds of government I should choose. I would infinitely prefer a limited monarchy, for I would sooner be the subject of the caprice of one man, than to the ignorance and passions of the multitude.

During this period other events also turned Webster to the right and away from his earlier pro-revolutionary zeal. He was deeply appalled by Shays's Rebellion in Massachusetts; more important, however, was his growing conviction that the United States was in need of a stronger federal union. This was the central point of his essay, *Sketches of American Policy*, written in 1785. Also very important in moderating Webster's earlier pro-revolutionary stance was his extensive tour of the United States undertaken to promote his schoolbooks and to distribute copies of his *Sketches* to influential people. He also

continued to seek copyright laws to protect his schoolbooks, especially in the South. The tour began in May 1785 and was a full-
blown example of Webster's faith in himself, his work, and his ability to promote both. For approximately eighteen months he traveled
to nearly every major city in the United States, lecturing on language
and seeking endorsements of his schoolbooks from prominent people
such as George Washington (who refused). That failure, however, did
not deter him; by the end of his trip his books were being printed
and read in nearly every part of the country.

Webster's journey was also tinged with nationalism. As he put it,
his lectures were an effort "to deliver literature and my countrymen
from the errors that fashion and ignorance are palming upon Englishmen." He believed that Americans should learn from American
books, but he was aware of sectional hostility and of the preference
Americans habitually showed for foreign authors. He felt that "two
circumstances operate against me. I am not a *foreigner;* I am a New
Englandman."13

He was both of these with a vengeance. His New England mind
was aghast when confronted with Southern life. The behavior of the
Southern elite and their love of gambling, horse racing, and expen-
sive parties led Webster to exclaim "O New England! How superior
are thy inhabitants in morals, literature, civility and industry."14 Yet
Webster, who clearly disliked the South, actually volunteered to remain in Virginia as tutor to George Washington's children. He wrote
Washington, "I wish to be settled in life. I wish not for solitude, but
to have it in my power to be retired. . . . Books and business will
ever be my principal pleasure. I must write: it is a happiness I cannot
sacrifice. . . ."15

Webster returned to Hartford for a brief time after his trip. His
journey had persuaded him that his ideas about language, education,
and politics were new and that he could be a leader of national opinion. Webster soon took an opportunity to be at the center of excite-
ment; he accepted a position teaching at the Episcopal Academy in
Philadelphia. This move took him to a major cosmopolitan city and
gave him a chance to hobnob with the delegates to the Constitutional
Convention (it also gave him a chance to ride on John Fitch's new
invention, the steamboat).

The Noah Webster who lived in Philadelphia during most of 1787
was a young man "on the make." His opinions frequently appeared
in Philadelphia papers and his style apparently offended some. An

anonymous writer complained in the *Freeman's Journal* about Webster's arrogant tone, unseemly in a mere schoolteacher. Webster's response revealed a personality growing more vain and self-possessed; he claimed that he was from one of

the oldest and most respected families in America, and his ancestors governed provinces fifty years before Pennsylvania was settled; that he received as good an education as America can afford, and improved it by personal acquaintance with the greater part of the literary gentlemen in the United States; that his grammatical publications are received into use in one half the States and are spreading in the others as fast as they can be published; that his *neglected* lectures have been, and still are, under the patronage of the first characters in America; that his political writings have been the acknowledged means of restoring federal measures of great consequence.[16]

It was all very true, if a bit overblown, and serves as a brief summary of Webster's life up to 1787. The statement, however, left out one important fact: Webster had not yet found the position that would provide a steady income and the prestige to make him a respected voice in national affairs. He had another reason for seeking a stable job; in Philadelphia he had met and fallen in love with Rebecca Greenleaf in the summer of 1787. This relationship revealed another side of Webster's personality. His letters to her before their marriage in October 1789 show his romantic and sentimental side in a way that he rarely if ever exhibited elsewhere (he also confessed that he was prone to depression and self-doubt). For example, his sentimentality was evident when, in June 1787, he sent Rebecca a lock of his hair which she was to keep "no longer than I deserve to be remembered." In the fall he wrote that "among other instances of my readiness to obey your wishes, you may rank the mode of dressing my hair. I have turned it back, and I think I look like a witch. . . . "
More important, he revealed to Rebecca his own thoughts about himself: "I suspect I am not formed for society; and I wait only to be convinced that people wish to get rid of my company, and I would leave them for better companions: the reflections of my own mind."[17] These letters revealed that Webster had great need for a wife like Rebecca and a regular family life. His family life was always a great comfort to him and it served as a peaceful retreat from the political passions and struggles after 1789.

Journalism and Federalist Politics

Before he could marry Rebecca, however, he had to establish himself so that he could support her properly. In November 1787 he moved to New York and founded the *American Magazine*. The magazine represented many things in Webster's life. It was his first attempt to earn a living outside the schoolroom and the courthouse. The magazine also gave him a forum in which to express his views on a number of issues, most often on education and politics. Although he worked incredibly hard on each issue, even his devotion could not keep the monthly journal from folding in less than a year; Webster lost £250 on the venture.

He returned to Hartford still seeking a steady position in the world. He returned to the law and wrote, publishing his lectures on language with additional material as *Dissertations on the English Language*. It did not sell and he lost more money; only a gift of a thousand dollars from Rebecca's wealthy brother, James, allowed Webster to marry Rebecca in October 1789.

His marriage into the Greenleaf family was an important event in his life. It drew him into a Boston family of considerable means and influence. James Greenleaf, Rebecca's brother, was a wealthy exporter who supplied Webster with crucial loans and contacts. Moreover, the marriage provided Webster with an impressive set of brothers-in-law. Thomas Dawes, married to Rebecca's sister Peggy, was a prominent Boston lawyer who later became a justice on the Massachusetts Supreme Court. Rebecca's sister Sally married Nathaniel Appleton, one of Boston's most prominent physicians. Both men were ardent Federalists who believed deeply in governance by an elite and in the development of a deferential populace. Webster became very close to Dawes and wrote some of his most revealing and philosophical letters to him. Appleton died in 1795, apparently before Webster could establish much of a relationship. The marriage, in the fullness of time, provided Webster with a thriving family life full of daughters: Emily born in 1790, Frances Juliana in 1793, Harriet in 1797, Eliza in 1803, and Louisa in 1808. Rebecca also bore two sons: William Greenleaf, born in 1801, survived his father as did all the daughters, but Henry Bradford, born in 1806, died shortly after birth.

By the early 1790s Webster had made a clean break with schoolteaching. He practiced law and wrote while in Hartford and served on the city council; he published a collection of his earlier essays in

1790, and in 1791 he published *The Prompter,* a series of meditations on common sayings, written in understated Yankee style. His schoolbooks continued to sell and began to provide him with a modest income. He devoted some of this income to publishing the *Journal* of John Winthrop, the first governor of the Massachusetts Bay Colony, whose manuscript Webster had come across at Governor Trumbull's house in Lebanon, Connecticut. The work of unlocking the mysteries of Winthrop's peculiar handwriting Webster farmed out to John Porter. This publishing venture netted Webster no profit, but it did bring him into close contact with a central source of Puritan thought.

In the summer of 1793 his life took a momentous turn. In July a group of Federalist Party leaders proposed that Webster edit a newspaper in New York City to oppose the *New York Journal,* a strong antifederalist paper. Webster was at a point in his life where such an offer was nearly irresistible. He was in debt from the failure of the *American Magazine,* from underwriting the printing of his own work, and reluctant to accept further gifts from his brother-in-law. His law practice produced little income and his royalties did not cover his debts. Noah needed a new business and he readily agreed to go to New York and edit the new paper.

In New York to close the deal, Webster found himself in the midst of the furor created by the arrival of the French ambassador Edmond Genet. As luck would have it, Webster lodged at Bradley's Tavern where Genet was also staying, and when the two met at dinner, for a few minutes the discussion was cordial. But soon Genet proclaimed that the United States was dominated by England. When one of Genet's aides remarked in French that "General Washington is making war on the French nation," Webster completely lost his temper; he asked Genet if he thought Washington and his aides were fools. The French envoy replied, "Mr. Jefferson is no fool." The remark left Webster sputtering with rage.[18]

The argument with Genet marked an important point in Webster's life. Genet and the whirling mobs of pro-French New Yorkers forced Webster to consider the significance of the French Revolution and its excesses. He had welcomed the revolt in France from the beginning but after 1793 he steadily withdrew his support. In the process he was forced to retreat even further from his earlier positions on revolution, republicanism, and the nature of man. He began to see the mobs of Paris and New York as a serious threat to liberty—as serious as an English or French king. In 1794 Webster published an essay on the French Revolution, which stands as a key to understanding his gradual turn away from a revolutionary, enlightened position and his transformation into a frightened, conservative Federalist.

This transformation, of course, rested on more than one run-in with a French ambassador. Webster, as an editor of a New York paper, was thrown into the political storms of the 1790s. Perhaps at no time in America's past had political debate employed so much slander and outright name-calling as during Webster's years as a newspaper editor (1793–1798). One of the central issues was America's position in world affairs. With revolutionary France and the European monarchies locked in a desperate struggle, both sides sought allies wherever they could find them. For Americans this was a most difficult dilemma since it also posed important questions about the nature of their own revolution. Should they side with France who had helped them in their own revolution or with England with whom they had just fought a bitter war? French revolutionary radicalism bothered many Americans who were influenced by the deep cultural and economic ties to England, while others saw France as extending the revolutionary movement begun in America. As the situation in Europe grew more violent, deep divisions developed in America; to some extent it became a sectional conflict with New England siding with Britain and much of the South siding with France. The Federalist government under Washington tried to remain neutral, and in response some Americans saw this as a betrayal of the 1778 alliance with France. Webster defended administration policy and the attacks came quickly from the pro-French critics of Washington's presidency. Webster's defense of the 1793 Neutrality Proclamation and Jay's Treaty earned him the scorn of editors such as Benjamin Franklin Bache who saw both measures as pro-English and a violation of American's duty to aid republican France in her struggle against the united monarchies of Europe.

Science, Religion, and Conservativism

Webster gave as good as he got during his years in New York. The battles wore him down, however, and the ceaseless toil required of an editor exhausted him. The constant attacks on his character also offended him. The newspaper battles of the 1790s collided with his vision of a deferential world where people like himself were not vilified daily in the press. His decision to retire from journalism in 1798 was based on a number of factors, but perhaps most important was the fact that, as Webster put it, ". . . . I found myself exposed to so many personal indignities from different parties that retirement was essential to my happiness if not my life. . . . to a gentlemen of my education and standing in society this treatment became intolerable."[19]

While retiring as editor, Webster kept his financial interest in the New York paper until 1803. By spring of 1798 he was back in New Haven researching and writing on the history of epidemic diseases. Webster had a lifelong interest in science. During his term as editor the epidemics that ravaged American cities were one of his major concerns; research begun in New York and continued in New Haven eventually served as the basis for Webster's main scientific contribution, *A Brief History of Epidemic and Pestilential Diseases . . .*, published in December 1799. While in New Haven he also served on the city council and in the state legislature.

Webster spent the next decade in Connecticut. After completing his work on epidemics, he turned to the labor that would occupy much of his energy for the rest of his life—the making of dictionaries. While he had conceived of the idea of an American dictionary in the 1780s, he did not begin the work until 1800. Webster produced a short work, the *Compendious Dictionary,* in 1806 and after years of toil published the unabridged version in 1828.

The Connecticut to which Webster retired was in turmoil. It was still a conservative state ruled by a long-standing elite of which Webster was a part. His Yale classmate, Oliver Wolcott, Jr., was governor and Webster's son-in-law, Chauncey Goodrich, who had married Frances, was a leading state senator. Webster's home in New Haven often welcomed visits from the powerful and influential men who ran Connecticut. At the same time, however, opposition to this elite was growing. Led in the beginning by another of Webster's Yale classmates, Abraham Bishop, Connecticut's Jeffersonian faction attacked the oligarchy and the powerful role played by the clergy and college in the state's politics. In essence, Webster found himself in the middle of a confrontation between an established Federalist elite and a challenging group of newcomers. There were all sorts of new pressures such as the influx of Irish immigrants who more often than not enlisted in the Jeffersonian party against the Federalists. Americans were also beginning their push across the Appalachians, and this diffusion of the population seemed to drain political power from Webster's New England.

As a result, like many Federalists after Jefferson's election in 1800,

Webster grew increasingly conservative and anxious. He saw the people more and more as a threat to liberty and a source of anarchy. In 1808 he made his views on the nature of man clear in a letter to Benjamin Rush: "As to mankind I believe the mass of them to be *copax rationis.* They are ignorant, or what is worse, governed by prejudices and authority—and the authority of men who flatter them instead of boldly telling them the truth."[20] In the same letter he proposed that the legal voting age be set at forty-five and that no man could hold office until he was fifty-five. After 1800, Webster was clearly a critic of the democratic movement symbolized by Jefferson's dramatic victory in 1800 and the rise of factional politics in Connecticut. He became, as part of a process that had begun in the mid-1780s, a defender of a worldview that featured, on the one hand, a negative opinion of the masses and, on the other, political and social leadership by an elite of older, well-educated men to whom strict deference was paid by the people.

These views clearly put him in the camp of the old-line Federalists who, as a group, grew steadily more anachronistic as the years passed. Yet Webster was in several ways at odds with this group; his insistence on American books for American minds ran counter to the beliefs of many old-guard Federalists who displayed an often slavish affection for British culture. The conflict centered around intellectual matters as well as politics. Many New England Federalists sought to preserve not only deferential politics but also a culture that resisted innovation. Webster's challenge to such British cultural touchstones as Samuel Johnson's dictionary drew the criticism of those who saw him tampering with eternal verities. Webster was aware of this criticism and the fact that it often alienated him from the elite. In 1802 he wrote that "either from the structure of my mind or from my modes of investigation, I am led very often to differ in opinion from many of my respectable fellow citizens, and differences of opinion is now a crime not easily overlooked or forgiven."[21] Thus, Webster was in some ways a typical Federalist, growing more negative and critical after 1800, but he escaped this stereotype because he continued to insist that Americans should reject the culture offered them by Europe and strive to create their own, even if this meant considerable innovation and change.

Between 1800 and 1808 Webster's religious beliefs radically changed. In his younger days he had said little about religion, but after 1800 it became a more profound influence on his life and thought. After 1808, religious feelings dominated his thoughts. At least as early as 1801 Webster was beginning to make room in his philosophy for a more active and omnipotent God. He wrote Samuel Mitchill that he had "no belief in the permanency of duration in any being but God and the operations of his power." He also claimed that "the result of my philosophy is to resolve every event and operation in the universe into the direct exertion of omnipotence."[22] These views are clearly a change from the opinion expressed in the 1780s that "God is love." During the years immediately after college he placed little emphasis on religion. At that time, he wrote Dawes, he doubted many basic Christian doctrines such as "regeneration, election, salvation by free grace, the atonement and the divinity of Christ . . . ."[23]

It is hard to pinpoint the factors that led to his conversion experience in 1808. The French Revolution and its radical religious innovations frightened him and led him to see the value of religion as a check on the passions of the people. Perhaps the religious controversy in the election of 1800 further entrenched the idea that a humbling religion with a strict moral code was necessary in a nation led by Thomas Jefferson whom Webster saw as immoral and atheistic. He was clearly pushed toward conversion by his wife and two eldest daughters who had been converted during a New Haven revival led by Reverend Moses Stuart.

The impact of his growing tendency to place more emphasis on religious matters was reflected in his relationship with Joel Barlow. Friends since college, Webster and Barlow remained close into the 1790s, but by 1798 Barlow's radical political views and his support of the religious innovations of the French Revolution had caused a breach in the friendship. Apparently the decline of the French threat and Barlow's return from Europe allowed the two men to resume their warm relationship. Religious differences, however, persisted and finally cooled the friendship. Webster wrote Barlow on 13 October 1808, that he had intended to publish a review of Barlow's poem *Columbiad,* but ill health and the religious principles of the poem prevented him from doing so. Webster claimed that "I cannot in a review omit to pass a severe censure on the atheistical principles it [the poem] contains" and that "no man on earth . . . had so large a share of my affections as Joel Barlow until you renounced the religion which you once preached and which I believe." Significantly, Webster hinted, in the same letter, that he had begun to suspect Barlow of harboring unorthodox religious views as early as 1792. Webster's turn toward more conventional Christian doctrine may well have begun around the same time.

Webster's growing religiosity and his conversion experience, however, may have had deeper roots. We know so little about his childhood that any speculation is difficult, but it is possible that his conversion in 1808 and the dominance of religious feeling in his thought after that point were the products of seeds sown in early life. Webster may have associated stability, order, and peace of mind with his childhood and his father's home in rural Connecticut. A central part of that world was an emphasis on a man's spiritual and religious success or failure. As late as 1782 his father and mother were still reminding him that a man's ultimate responsibility and duty was to God:

I wish to have you serve your generation and do good in the world and be useful and may so behave as to gain the esteem of all virtuous people that are acquainted with you and gain a comfortable subsistence, but especially that you may live as to obtain the favor of Almighty God and his grace in this world and a Saving interest in the merits of Jesus Christ, without which no man can be happy.[24]

Any psychological speculation about the past is risky but it is fair to assume that Webster never really forgot these parental expectations and that they played a role in his turn to religion.

Whatever the cause, Webster moved slowly toward a conversion experience. At first he fought the pull of religious emotionalism. Intellectually, he compared the creed accepted by his wife and daughters with his Episcopal beliefs; next he talked with Moses Stuart who removed many of his objections to Calvinist doctrines. Webster could not decide. He tried to work on his dictionary, but "at all times of the day and in the midst of other occupations I was suddenly seized with impressions, which called my mind irresistibly to religious concerns."

The final step came after religious impressions totally blocked his studies:

My mind was suddenly arrested, without any previous circumstances of the time to draw it to this subject as it were fastened to the awakening and upon my own conduct. I closed my books, yielded to the influence which could not be resisted or mistaken and was led by a spontaneous impulse to repentance, prayer and entire submission and surrender of myself to my maker and redeemer. My submission appeared to be cheerful and was soon followed by the peace of mind which the world can neither give nor take away.[25]

Thus Webster came to be counted among the many converted during the Second Great Awakening. From 1808 until his death, religion and the idea of an omnipotent Calvinist deity were all-important elements in his life and work. As he grew older, he constantly sought to employ religion as a device to control the passions of the people. Never again would he believe that secular education and correct politics could structure a stable state; a profound fear of a demanding God and strict religious moral training became basic tenets of his thought.

Webster had enlisted in the army of the converted along with a great number of his fellow citizens. The Great Revival, or the Second Great Awakening, was a fundamental event in American life. Well under way by 1800, the revival took aim at what it saw as the rise of skepticism, deism, and French influence. In New England it was able to effect a reunion of the Old Calvinists and the New Divinity groups who had been debating each other since the First Great Awakening in the 1740s. The renewed unity of Calvinist evangelicalism led to impressive new periodicals such as *The Panoplist* in 1805 and new schools such as the Andover Seminary in 1808. Yale, Princeton, and Andover began to produce missionaries who went off to Africa, India, and the American West. The great aim of the New England revival was to promote a redefined Calvinism and to instill in Americans a hatred of radical or liberal religion, a love of social order, and deference to a learned elite.

The Calvinism of 1810 was indeed a softened version of the seventeenth-century variety. The harsh doctrines of election and the innate depravity of man were trimmed and redefined to suit Americans less inclined to think badly of themselves. Yet nineteenth-century evangelical Calvinism retained at least one basic point of similarity with its seventeenth-century parent. In 1812 Lyman Beecher, one of the crucial figures in New England Calvinism, expressed that point in the simplest terms: "Our fathers were not fools; they were as far from it as modern philosophers are from wisdom. Their fundamental maxim was that a man is desperately wicked, and cannot be qualified for good membership in society without the influence of moral restraint."[26] The revival (and Webster) sought to create that moral restraint by forming countless organizations devoted to checking man's passions. They formed groups to promote temperance and to start Sunday Schools, and soon what had once been largely a negative movement was becoming a reform movement aiming at the moral perfection of America. While Webster may have found comfort and peace in his religious conversion, the revival that induced it hardly could have met with his approval. Like many developments in America between 1789 and 1840, the Great Revival aimed at order and control and it may, in part, have achieved this purpose, but it also led to more disquieting contention between groups and more social and political conflict.[27]

Webster had found God, but he had not found financial security. His schoolbooks produced a small income, and he had made a profit on the sale of his newspaper holdings, but the Embargo and the impending war had made life economically difficult for many New Englanders. So in 1812 Webster and his family left New Haven seeking a cheaper place to live; they settled in Amherst, Massachusetts, where they remained for a decade. Webster purchased a large double house with ten acres of good land where he planted an orchard and grew all the vegetables the family could eat. He indulged his love of scientific experimentation and published reports in *The Hampshire Gazette* on potatoes, fertilizers, and forest conservation. In these reports he revealed the deep bias he had for the agrarian life. He was especially fond of comparing the simple, American farmer with those who acquired property "by commercial speculations." Among all the other things Webster was, he was also a genuine agrarian who wanted Americans tilling the soil and shunning the sin of the cities.[28]

Webster quickly became an important figure in Amherst. He represented the town in the state legislature, and he also became involved in the founding of Amherst College. He worked endlessly to raise the funds and pass the legislation necessary to get the college on its feet. His newfound evangelical piety was a primary motivation for his interest in the new school. Amherst, in Webster's vision, would train missionaries who would carry the message of Jesus Christ to all corners of the globe and, equally important, for Webster at least, Amherst would teach Calvinist doctrine and help check the spread of the Unitarian creed emanating from Harvard College.

While in Amherst, Webster also became involved in the Hartford Convention. The War of 1812 was a severe hardship on New England, and Webster, like many New Englanders, saw President Madison as a Southerner willing to sacrifice the interests of New England. The national government had also shown remarkable ineptitude in fighting the war. By 1814, as gloom and despair settled over New England, some of its most prominent citizens began to entertain the idea of a meeting to discuss the section's grievances. A meeting of Massachusetts gentlemen discussed this idea and approved it on 19 January 1814. Webster was appointed to the committee charged with drafting a circular letter calling for delegates to a formal convention to deal with New England's grievances. The letter made it clear that Webster and the others saw their problems as rooted in much more than the temporary dislocations of war. They pointed to the disproportionate power held by the South, claiming this power was based on the right to count three of every five slaves as a person when determining representation in the national legislature. The letter also condemned the Congress for assuming the right to lay a trade embargo, a right, they claimed, reserved to the states.

After helping to draft the letter, Webster promoted the idea of a special sectional convention in a number of ways. He ran for the state assembly on a pro-convention platform and won easily although he barely met the residence requirements. Gradually, support for the idea proposed in the circular letter grew until finally during the last months of the war a convention was held. Although Webster was not chosen as a delegate and did not attend, he did defend the Hartford Convention against its critics for the rest of his life. He approved of it because, in his view, the convention reflected the desires of the people as represented in their assemblies. Webster was particularly vocal in defending the convention against the charge that it sought to undo the Union. He called this "a gross calumny, originating in mere surmise and party jealousy."[29]

The Dictionary

Webster was busy founding Amherst College and promoting the Hartford Convention and he was also devoted to the making of a dictionary. That, clearly, was his major task during the years at Amherst and after. As he worked on the project he constantly encountered roadblocks that required him to learn a new language or track the history of a crucial word. Feeling that he could not write the dictionary without long training in etymology, he suspended work on the dictionary and spent approximately ten years exploring ancient languages. He labored under terrific handicaps. First of all, many essential books were impossible to obtain in the United States, let alone in Amherst. Second, he lacked intellectual contact with people who could help him feel his way into new areas of study. Finally, he suffered from lack of money. He barely had enough to sustain his family and was forced to solicit aid from the wealthy.

By 1822 Webster's work on the dictionary reached a dead end. He had simply exhausted his own library and had come to see the necessity of a research trip to Europe. To prepare for the trip to England and France, he moved his family back to New Haven where Chauncey Goodrich, his son-in-law, could look after both Webster's family and business affairs while he was in Europe. After receiving an honorary Doctor of Laws degree from Yale, and with a thousand dollars borrowed from his daughter Harriet, Webster sailed for Europe in June 1824.

Webster's response to Europe was mixed. He was overwhelmed by the sight of 800,000 books at the Bibliothèque du Roi in Paris. No American library had 20 percent of such a collection. On the other hand, like a true American, Webster reported his shock at the deplorable conditions that European city dwellers endured. Webster, and his son William, who accompanied him on the trip, found "the morals of the greater part of the population . . . wretchedly depraved."[30]

After a stay in Paris, Noah and William traveled to Cambridge, England. Webster labored prodigiously in the libraries of the old English university. Ironically, the dictionary that was to be American and to help Americans end their dependence on English authorities was completed in England. Webster recalled the moment:

I finished writing my dictionary in January, 1825, at my lodgings in Cambridge, England. When I came to the last word I was seized with a trembling, which made it somewhat difficult to hold my pen steady for writing. The cause seems to have been the thought that I might not live to finish the work, or the thought that I was so near the end of my labors. But I summoned strength to finish the last word, and then walking about the room a few minutes, I recovered.[31]

Back in the United States, Sherman Converse agreed to publish the dictionary; however, Webster had to agree to underwrite some of the cost himself. In November 1828, after long hours of proofreading

and correcting, *An American Dictionary of the English Language* reached
the public.

The years after Webster published the dictionary were both bitter
and productive. Webster remained a disillusioned Federalist in a nation experiencing the trauma of rapid social and political change. He
wrote that if "Vermont would remain firm to the old Federalist principles, I should be tempted to remove to that state, to be freed from
our democracy. . . . We deserve all our public evils. We are a de-
generate and wicked people."[32]

He never stopped expressing himself on the issues of the day. The
campaign of 1840, for example, confirmed his view that politics had
degenerated steadily since Jefferson. "But the Log Cabin—oh how
the country is degraded, when ever men of respectability resort to
such means to secure an election! I struggled, in the days of Washington, to sustain good principles—but since Jefferson's principles
have prostrated the popular respect for sound principles, further efforts would be useless."[33]

To his credit, Webster knew he had changed. He wrote in 1835
that, as a young man, he had been "full of confidence in my own
opinions" but he had found many of those views "to be visionary and
deceptive." As his most recent biographer put it, "Noah Webster's
long journey ended in disillusionment, bitterness, and despair."[34]

Yet his last years produced a bountiful crop. He continued to support copyright legislation. In 1832 Webster published his *History of
the United States*. Approximately a year later he published a revised
version of the Bible, a work he considered the most important of his
life. The second edition of the unabridged dictionary appeared in
1841. In addition, Webster's views turned up regularly in the pages
of conservative newspapers. In May 1843, the month he died, Webster published a collection of his essays and papers.

Certain themes dominate any summary of Webster's life. First, his
life was marked by the classic transition from youthful, revolutionary
zeal to pessimistic authoritarianism in his later years. Profoundly af-
fected by a growing religious tenor of mind, he lost almost entirely
his faith in the people and in progress. Near the end of his life he
was convinced that America had gone astray and that submission to
an omnipotent God was the way to national salvation—he was afraid
the nation would not take that route. In the long run, his New England childhood proved to be a controlling force. He had absorbed the
religious, social, and intellectual traditions of nearly a century and a

half of New England Protestant thought, and neither his years at Yale nor the exhilarating radicalism of a revolutionary age could overcome the deep conservative influence of a Connecticut farm childhood—a childhood that deeply ingrained beliefs in deference to an elite, hard work, virtue, and obedience to God and to an absolute moral code. Yet he was unmistakably changed by the Enlightenment and the American Revolution. His belief in progress and scientific research, at the very least, kept him from making a total retreat into the past. Furthermore, he was a vain man fond of self-promotion. He believed that an elite should govern not only politically but culturally as well. He worked incessantly to join that elite. He was one of the first to understand that post-revolutionary America would be shaped by the opinions of the people and that books, pamphlets, and newspapers would shape that opinion. From the early 1780s Webster made it his task to become one of those chosen to write the words that would influence the nation. He never totally relinquished his youthful faith that he could change the minds of the young and the old. To the very end of his life he published his work so that the public might read it and be improved. Beneath the vanity and presumption there were doubts and, as he pushed forward, there was also an element in his personality that told him to withdraw. His wife and family served as a haven from the battle. Given the unhappy relations with his father and a long history of failure after college, perhaps Webster found it necessary to seal off his domestic life from the world of controversy and conflict that was so much a part of him.

Finally, Webster was a worker. He was capable of almost ceaseless toil. Why did he work so hard? For one thing, he inherited the belief in the worthiness of hard work from his New England ancestors. He also seemed compelled to seek status and recognition and worked tirelessly to get it. His writings are hardly art: they are the product of a man, a tradesman in words, seeking influence and station.

Chapter Two

Schoolbooks, Schoolhouses, and Moralisms

As a young man, Noah Webster was forced into schoolteaching. Education in the United States was in a sorry state, or at least Webster thought so. The teachers were often ill suited to their task, the schoolhouses were cold, uncomfortable places, and the schoolbooks were old and unsuitable for revolutionary America—written, more often than not, by Englishmen. Webster saw all this in the early 1780s and set out to change it. He transformed his teaching experience from a cruel necessity into the basis for a lifelong career as an author of textbooks and a theorizer on education. Webster, more than anyone else, deserves the title "schoolmaster of America."

His contribution to education cannot be overestimated. It rests primarily on his *Spelling Book*. This little book, which taught millions of Americans to spell, sold more copies and influenced more young lives than any other secular book in American history. Linked with the speller were two other basic texts—a grammar and a reader. Webster planned the three books as a set and gave them the grand title *A grammatical institute, of the English language, comprising, an easy, concise, and systematic method of education, designed for the use of English schools in America. In three parts.*[1] The grammar and the reader, however, never matched the popularity of the speller and the idea of the three as a set died in the early nineteenth century.

On several occasions during his career Webster recorded his thoughts on the theory of education. As a young man caught up in the fluid world of revolutionary America, he saw education as a means of severing cultural ties with England and as a way of establishing a uniquely American character. As he grew older, however, education became for Webster less an agent of change and more a tool of social control. Early in his career Webster made little room in his curriculum for religion, but later, especially after his own conversion in 1808, he included more and more religious and moral training in his ideal education for America's young people.

The Speller

An American schoolchild in the nineteenth century was likely to have as his or her first text Webster's *Spelling Book:* "The back of the cover is of coarse linen clothe—very coarse—threads within sight of each other. The sides of the cover are of layers of brown paper, with an over-all of thin blue paper. The paper and pages within look as if they might have come from a mill using bleached straw and slacked lime, with a little sulphur thrown in to give it tinting."[2] The publishing history of this little book is very complicated. There were four versions of the speller. The book appeared originally in 1783; Webster revised it in 1787 and changed the name to *The American Spelling Book.* In 1804 Webster, once again, revised the volume slightly and took out a new copyright. In 1829 he completed the last revision and changed the name again, this time to *The Elementary Spelling Book.* This brief summary hardly does justice to the complexity and confusion surrounding the history of this simple little book. Webster's bibliographer lists 388 printings of one kind or another between 1783 and Webster's death in 1843. Printers changed the text without permission and continued to print outdated versions long after Webster had issued a revised text. This was especially true of *The American Spelling Book* which lived on long after *The Elementary Spelling Book* appeared.

Whatever the form, the speller was a popular book. The first edition of five thousand copies sold out in nine months, and printers quickly began to run off new editions to supply their local demand. More than fifty editions were issued before 1800, more than a hundred before 1814, and more than one hundred fifty by 1829. By one estimate, approximately one hundred million copies of the speller were sold. This is probably a conservative estimate since it takes no account of bootleg issues and purposeful overruns by licensed printers who reported a much smaller number of copies than were actually printed.

Webster had produced the book that could have made him a fortune. A small royalty on each copy sold would have made him a rich man, but Webster, always in need of money, rarely took royalties; instead, he sold the rights to print the work for lump sums. For example, he sold the unlimited rights to print the speller for five years in New York, New Jersey, North and South Carolina, and Georgia for two hundred dollars. The printer, Samuel Campbell, sold twenty thousand copies a year and ran off one hundred thousand just before his license ran out. In this instance, selling his interest in the work outright cost Webster approximately twenty-five hundred dollars, an immense sum at the time. Such an arrangement was not uncommon; one of Webster's account books listed over one hundred printers and publishers who had purchased the rights to print the speller in their districts.

During its life as America's spelling book, Webster's work was altered to fit local conditions and historical changes. Nothing illustrates this adaption so well as the appearance of specialized editions for the South. In 1863, for example, Robert Fleming of Georgia obtained a copyright for *The Elementary Spelling Book Revised and adapted to the Youth of the Southern Confederacy, interspersed with Bible Readings on Domestic Slavery.*

Given the multitude of editions and the four basic revisions by Webster, it is impossible to provide a description of the speller that takes into account all of its guises. The basic structure of the book remained the same. The speller first introduced the student to the letters of the alphabet and the sounds of these letters. After the student had committed the alphabet to memory, he moved on to tables of nonsense syllables of two and three letters. After mastering these sounds, he graduated to tables of words. Webster arranged words into tables by association. For example, he grouped seventy-two words into one table labeled "Easy words of four syllables, the full accent on the first, and the half accent on the third." Thus, the student pronounced from a table that included "in-vent-o-ry," "ad-ver-sa-ry" and "tes-ti-mo-ny."[3] By the middle of the book the tables of words began to give way to reading lessons of increasing difficulty. In most editions the first sentence a student read was "No man may put off the law of God: / My joy is in his law all the day." Toward the end, the speller began to take on the quality of an encyclopedia, presenting tables that bristled with geographical information. Like the word lists earlier in the text, Webster put towns, cities, rivers, and countries together by association. For example, the table headed by the note that "the following have the accent on the second syllable" included "A-las-ka," "Ca-taw-ba," "Ha-van-na" and "Mi-am-i." In many editions Webster attached a "catechism" to the text. Before 1800 this was a "Federal Catechism," but this political message gave way to "A Moral Catechism" in most nineteenth-century editions. In some cases both catechisms were included.

Of all the changes Webster made, perhaps the most popular was the inclusion of a series of fables in editions after 1787. The most popular ones were "Of the Boy that Stole Apples," "The Country Maid and her Milk Pail," "The Partial Judge," and "Two Dogs." This last fable was the sad story of a good dog who took up with an evil mongrel. They entered a village and the evil one attacked a town dog, and when the villagers responded they hurled their stones at both dogs. The moral, that one should pick friends from among the virtuous, was clear to the youthful readers.

Students may have agonized over the spelling drills but, if they enjoyed anything, they enjoyed, and remembered, the fables. The following is the complete text of "Of the Boy that Stole Apples," one of the most popular fables:

An old Man found a rude Boy upon one of his trees stealing Apples, and desired him to come down; but the young Sauce-box told him plainly he would not. Won't you? said the old Man, then I will fetch you down; so he pulled up some tufts of Grass and threw at him; but this only made the Youngster laugh, to think the old Man should pretend to beat him down from the tree with grass only.

Well, well, said the old Man, if neither words nor grass will do, I must try what virtue there is in stones: so the old Man pelted him heartily with stones, which soon made the young chap hasten down from the tree and beg the old Man's pardon.

MORAL

If good words and gentle means will not reclaim the wicked, they must be dealt with in a more severe manner.

The fables, such as the one above, and the other little stories made the speller a moral tract. Students remembered the agony of memorizing the alphabet and learning to spell long lists of strange words. More important, they remembered the moral lessons. Chase Osborn, the governor of Michigan, recalled that the reading assignments in the speller "had almost the standing of the Ten Commandments."[4] Alongside the Bible and the church stood Webster's blue-backed spelling book, all seeking to teach basic Christian ethics to a growing nation.

The moralistic tone in the speller was the product of two causes. As a New Englander, Webster carried with him a full measure of the Protestant ethic and this passed easily into his textbooks. For example, the speller, in its reading lessons and in the "Moral Catechism," rarely missed a chance to urge thrift. Many editions contained the lesson, "Domestic Economy, or, the History of Thrifty and Unthrifty." In his homily students learned that one of the chief differences between men was "that one man spends only the *interest* of his money, while the other spends the *principal*." The story contrasts "Thrifty," a hard-working farmer, with "Unthrifty," a poorly organized slugabed and drinker. The "Moral Catechism" contained a whole section on frugality and economy, another on industry, and still another on avarice. On the whole, the ethical lessons that students learned from Webster's text were not a great deal different than those the same student might have learned in the early eighteenth century.[5]

This continuity is not surprising since Webster took much of the spelling book from early schoolbooks printed in more religious times. He borrowed heavily from two works by English authors: *The Universal Spelling Book* (1756) by Daniel Fenning and *The New Guide to the English Tongue* (1740) by Thomas Dilworth. In addition to imitating both works' use of the Psalms as reading lessons, Webster borrowed the "Story of Tommy and Harry" from Fenning, and Webster's first reading lesson in the first edition was clearly copied from Dilworth.

> *Dilworth*
> No man may put off the law of God
> The way of God is no ill way
> My joy is in God all the Day
> A bad man is a Foe to God
>
> *Webster*
> No man may put off the law of God
> My joy is in his law all the day
> O may I not go in the way of sin
> Let me not go in the way of ill men[6]

A comparison of the two reading lessons shows Webster's tendency to secularize slightly the material he borrowed. He was caught in a more rationalistic age, and his work bears the mark of this age, yet he managed, much like Benjamin Franklin whom he admired, to color his work with the moral maxims of his more religious forebears.

The speller was much more than a school text and a moral lesson book. Through it Webster sought to create a national language that would serve as a basic link between the various religious, ethnic, and sectional groups that were confronted with the task of making one nation out of thirteen colonies. For him, one of the basic purposes of the speller was

to diffuse an uniformity and purity of language in America—to destroy the provincial prejudices that originate in the trifling differences of dialect, and produce reciprocal ridicule—to promote the interest of literature and harmony of the United States—is the most ardent wish of the Author; and it is his highest ambition to deserve the approbation and encouragement of his countrymen.[7]

Webster's nationalism surfaced in several other ways. First of all, in many editions he included footnotes that warned against linguistic "improprieties, introduced by settlers from various parts of Europe. . . ." Specifically, he suggested "chimney" rather than "chimbley," "cover" rather than "kiver," and "raspberry" not "rozberry." Second, he replaced the English and European place names he found in Dilworth with American names. But his nationalism was tinted with provincialism. In early editions of the speller he listed the principal towns of Connecticut and their distance from Hartford. Such localism tended to disappear as the speller gained a national audience. Third, Webster promoted his little book by appealing to the rising nationalistic and anti-European bias in the new nation. He saw the speller as part of a declaration of cultural independence. He saw clearly that "America must be as independent in *literature* as she is in *politics,* as famous for *arts* as for *arms*. . . ."[8] The obvious starting point for American cultural independence was with young children just learning to spell and read.

In Webster's vision of America the speller had a significant social role to play. Webster was attempting to touch as many people as possible with his spelling book. He had made a choice to write for the masses and not for the elite. In a letter to John Canfield, a Connecticut legislator, he compared his schoolbook with a work upon "some abstruse philosophical subject"; the latter, he concluded, would be read by only a few and "gives light only in the chamber of study . . . while a little fifteen-penny volume . . . casts its beams equally upon the peasant and the monarch."[9] Thus, Webster reflected a fundamental tenet of post-revolutionary ideology. When he was writing his first texts nothing seemed more important to the future of America than the people's ability to handle their newly won freedom. A virtuous and moral population was the key to a stable republic while fear of unruly masses armed with political power lurked in the minds of men like Webster. The spelling book with its strong moral tone and its nationalistic call for linguistic unity was Webster's contribution to the creation of a populace steeped in virtue and republican piety.

Finally, while Webster's spelling book was clearly a call to cultural independence and national pride, it was also something more. A careful reading of his introduction to the 1783 edition reveals the unmistakable signs of an anxious man. The little spelling book he had written was designed to play a role in a great drama. As the revolution ended, Americans began to fragment into quarreling groups. In almost every state one found evidence that postwar America would be disrupted by petty conflicts and an excessive emphasis on the equality of all men. Webster, imbued with the notion that the New World must be an example to the Old, felt that unity was essential. America must present one face to the rest of the world, and in this context every issue, even language, became a symbol of American success or failure. Thus, language was too important to be left "to parents and nurses, to ignorance and caprice, to custom, accident, or nothing— nay, to coxcombs, who have a large share in directing the *polite taste* of pronunciation, which of course is as vicious as that of any other class of people." If left to these random influences, "every person will claim a right to pronounce most agreably [*sic*] to his own fancy, and the language will be exposed to perpetual fluctuation." Such a state of affairs would indicate the lack of virtue among Americans; they must give up their willy-nilly approach to language and speech and assemble peaceably under one uniform language laid out for them in Webster's speller.

Scholars have usually emphasized the nationalism and the stress on cultural independence in the spelling book. They have not, however, stressed that both were caused in part by Webster's anxiety over the fragmentation and disunity of the American people in the early 1780s. Once we recognize this, we can realize the importance of stable authority to Webster, even in his early years. The speller was only the first of many attempts in education, politics, language, religion, and science to vanquish the reality of division and conflict and to establish a single standard, a uniformity, an order to things. In a revolutionary world the tide of history was against him and, after 1783, divisions became deeper and conflicts more bitter. In response, Webster sought out stronger sources of authority to bring all Americans together again.

The Grammar

In 1784 Webster published the second part of his *Grammatical Institute*. It never approached the popularity of the speller and died quietly before the nineteenth century had hardly begun. After the first edition appeared in 1784, approximately forty-four editions were subsequently printed—the majority of them before 1800. Webster's four revisions sought the formula that would link his grammar with his speller in the public mind, but he never found it. In 1795 Lindley Murray published *English Grammar, Adapted to Different Classes of Learners*, and this work pushed Webster and others from the field. Murray's work dominated grammar instruction much as Webster's did spelling.

Like the speller, the grammar was not an entirely original work. Webster freely admitted that he had drawn heavily on Robert Lowth's (1710–1787) *A Short Introduction to Grammar*. Lowth's influence, as professor of poetry at Oxford and later as bishop of London, was extensive in the eighteenth century. He began the process of untangling English grammar from Latin rules. Webster reflected this tendency in the preface of his grammar:

We are apt to be surprised, that men who made the languages their principal study, and during their whole lives, were employed in teaching youth, should not discover that the grammar of one language would not answer for another; but our wonder will cease when we reflect, that the English nation at large has, till very lately, entertained the idea that our language was incapable of being reduced to a system of rules; and that even now many . . . contend that the only way of acquiring a grammatical knowledge of the *English Tongue* is first to learn a *Latin Grammar*. [10]

Webster, however, was himself unable to escape the influence of Latin. For one thing, his text followed the classical organizational scheme used by Latin grammars. Part II of the *Institute* begins with a summary of the speller—the ABCs, syllables, and words. It then goes on to introduce the parts of speech and their definitions. The remainder of the text consists of drills based on the age-old methods of teaching Latin—memorization, parsing, and the correction of false syntax. The student, following a question-and-answer format, had the parts of speech and grammatical rules drilled into his head by endless repetition. Then came parsing drills, a form of torture by which the student was given a statement (often one sentence, but sometimes more) to break down into its component parts of speech with an explanation of the form, function, and syntactical relationship of each part. Correcting syntax was perhaps more fun than parsing. The student was given a sentence, often from Shakespeare, Dryden, or Pope, and told to correct it. For example, Dryden's sentence, "She not denies it," should be rewritten "She denies it not," according to Webster. Webster also included examples from the Bible for correction, anticipating his 1833 revision of the Scriptures in which he attempted to make the Bible conform to his idea of proper usage.

In constructing a grammar Webster took a stand on several issues that illustrate the fluidity of language in his time. For instance, he maintained that "you was" was correct, even when "you" referred to an individual. He also condemned the phrase "what is the news" as incorrect. However, in the 1787 edition he contended that "anomalous phrases creep into languages, in its infancy; and become established idioms. . . . On this principle we admit these expressions . . . *you are,* applied to an individual; *this news is favorable,* and many other expressions in our language."[11] Such shifting of opinions and general uncertainty probably contributed to the relative lack of success of the grammar text.

Webster's inconsistency was graphically illustrated when he came under the influence of the language theories of Horne Tooke. In 1787 he read Tooke's *The Diversions of Purley* (1786). Tooke was something of a hero in America; he had been fined and imprisoned by the British for raising money to aid widows and orphans of men killed at Lexington and Concord. After his release, he retired to his country estate, Purley near Surrey, and carried on discussions of the language with friends. The *Diversions* amount to transcripts of those discussions. Tooke abandoned Latin entirely and came to see Anglo-Saxon as the root of English. This theory led him to reject Lowth's grammar upon which Webster had based so much of his own. Webster was convinced by Tooke that Part II of the *Institute* was substantially incorrect.

In 1807, after years of research, guided by Tooke's principles, Webster published *A Philosophical and Practical Grammar of the English*

Language. In this work he put forth two basic theories. He held that Anglo-Saxon provided "legitimate principles and established usages" for modern English and that indeclinable words in English were derived from declinable ones. The 1807 grammar was different from his earlier work in other ways. Among other things he took exception to standard grammatical terms. He used *attribute* for *adjective, connective* for *conjunction,* and for *pronoun* he suggested *substitute.*

The *Philosophical and Practical Grammar* did not meet with much success, even after a shortened version was attached to the *American Dictionary* in 1828. Webster produced a grammar text in 1831, but it died quickly in the contest with more established texts. Webster was never to make much of an impact on the study of grammar. He changed his views often, and as the nineteenth century grew older, his theories grew eccentric. But he wrote the first grammar text to be widely employed in America and no doubt drew more competent grammarians into the field. Finally, his constant attacks against the influence of Latin grammar may have helped bring on the day when Latin and English grammar parted company.

The Reader

The third and last part of the *Grammatical Institute* was a reader composed of selections for the student to read and, in some cases, to speak aloud. The reader took the title *An American Selection . . .* in 1787 and was generally known by that name. It was somewhat more popular than the grammar, but somewhat less widely used than the speller. Webster's bibliographer records almost eighty editions of this work. Other readers, such as Caleb Bingham's *American Preceptor* (1794) and Lindley Murray's *English Reader* (1799), took the pattern Webster had helped to establish for the reader and constructed more popular ones.

The book had two sections. In the first Webster presented rules for reading and speaking. They amount to common sense: advising the student to speak clearly; to pause at the proper places; to pay attention to cadence, accent, and emphasis; and to use the proper gestures to express sentiments. After the introduction of these rules, the student found "General Directions for expressing certain Passions or Sentiments." The young reader was expected to learn the proper "look" (facial expression, body position, and tone) for a long list of emotions. For example:

Authority opens the countenance, but draws down the eyebrows a little, so as to give the person an air of authority.

Wonder opens the eyes, and makes them appear prominent. The body is fixed in a contracted stooping posture, the mouth is open, the hands often raised. Wonder at first strikes a person dumb; then breaks forth into exclamations.

Malice sets the jaws, or gnashes the teeth, sends flashes from the eyes, draws the mouth down towards the ears, clenches the fist, and bends the elbows.

Mirth or *Laughter* opens the mouth, crisps the nose, lessens the aperture of the eyes, and shakes the whole frame.

Perplexity . . . suddenly the whole body is agitated, the person walks about busily, stops abruptly, talks to himself, etc.[12]

After learning the rules, the student passed on to the actual reading and speaking of various selections. Often these selections were keyed to one of the emotions. Frequently the readings were excerpts from plays, an interesting phenomenon since drama was a form of literature that Webster frequently criticized as immoral and vulgar. To teach cadence and the use of proper emphasis Webster included lines of poetry and often marked the passages so that the young reader would know which words to emphasize ("To *err* is human; to *forgive, divine*"). The remainder of the book, and by far the largest portion, was composed of selections calculated to instill patriotism, religion, and morality.

Webster's devotion to American nationalism was perhaps more clearly expressed in the reader than in the speller or grammar. In the preface to the 1785 edition Webster wrote one of his most often quoted statements: "For America in her infancy to adopt the present maxims of the Old World would be to stamp the wrinkle of decrepit old age upon the bloom of youth, and to plant the seed of decay in a vigorous constitution" (*AS,* iv). Consistent with this call for an American culture free of European influences, Webster selected readings with a preference for things American. He included Philip Freneau's "On General Washington," Joseph Warren's "Oration on the Boston Massacre," and John Hancock's "The Declaration of Independence." In the various editions about one third of the reading selections were patriotic pieces. Furthermore, Webster wrote pieces of his own on American geography, the settlement of the New World, and the Revolutionary War.

Nationalism and patriotism were certainly not more important than morality, manners, and religion. In this Webster clearly reflected the age in which he lived. All of the readers that gained any popularity had a strong moral and religious tone, but the movement was away from an overwhelming emphasis on religious matters such as the Christian view of death, immortality, and sin. Instead, Webster's reader took a much more generalized attitude toward religion, often suggesting to students that they accept the existence of a higher Being who controlled their lives. For example, the following sentence was among those included "to form the morals of youth": "There is but one way of fortifying the soul against all gloomy presages and terrors of the mind, and that is, by securing to ourselves the friendship and protection of that Being who disposes of events and governs futurity" (*AS*, 93). This sentiment would have been out of place in earlier seventeenth-century readers, such as *The New England Primer*, with their gloomy emphasis on death and the iron hand of an all-powerful deity.

While religion was de-emphasized, manners and morals were not. As in the speller, Webster's reader constantly sought to instruct youth on cleanliness, deportment, and the proper role of young people in society. In this regard, one of the most interesting reading lessons was "Character of a Young Lady." The story of Sophia was, in fact, a lesson to young girls on the proper role of women. "Sophia is not a beauty," but we learn that "in her presence, beauties are discontented with themselves. She dresses well but despises finery and fashion. As a young girl Sophia's main obligation is to her father and mother." Her "understanding is solid without being profound." The "ruling passion" of Sophia's life is "the love of virtue . . . because it is the glory of the female sex. . . . Without much knowledge of the world . . . she seeks only to please and fulfill the obligations of a woman" (*AS* [Hartford, 1807], 29–30).

Often included in the reader was a selection entitled "Rules for Behavior" (mostly from Lord Chesterfield but modified by Webster). The rules were arranged in a series of separate sentences that were read in order by various students in class. The result must have been much like a grammar drill on personal deportment and habits. The rules assumed that the student knew little about manners and personal grooming, suggesting that Webster, by including this section, hoped that the school could aid the family in the training of children in the basics of life. There were countless rules concerning cleanliness such as "be attentive to neatness . . . a dirty mouth is not only dis-agreeable, as it occasions an offensive breath, but almost infallibly causes a decay and loss of teeth." Much of the advice was negative; Webster urged students to avoid "loud laughter," "humming," "drumming your fingers," "whistling," "staring full in the face," "impertinent curiosity," and "bashfulness." He included several rules for governing social discourse; he advised "never hold any body by the button or hand, in order to be heard through your story; for if people are not willing to hear you, you had much better hold your tongue, than hold *them*" (*AS,* 65, 67).

"Rules for Behavior" occasionally went beyond advice on manners. As in most of Webster's schoolbooks, the student was urged to prac-tice thrift. Young Americans learned from Webster that "a wise man employs his money, as he does his time—he never spends a shilling of the one, nor a minute of the other, but in something either useful or rationally pleasing. The fool buys what he does not want, but does not pay for what he stands in need." The selection concluded with what was a standard theme in all American readers—"Above all, ad-here to morals and religion, with immoveable firmness" (*AS,* 69–70).

The story of Sophia and "Rules for Behavior" were typical of most of the reading lessons in *An American Selection.* They sought to instill in their readers basic lessons about proper values, roles, and manners. Webster's reader was not unique, it was only one of many that guarded tradition in the post-revolutionary world. These texts were a conservative force in a nation undergoing great political, intellec-tual, and social change. Since Webster was the first American to ven-ture into the making of schoolbooks for his countrymen, one of his most important achievements was to help establish basic school texts as defenders of the old values.

History of the United States

During his long life Webster produced a number of different text-books in addition to the three parts of the *Grammatical Institute.* None of them achieved anything like wide use. In 1802 he published *Ele-ments of Useful Knowledge;* in 1830 *Biography for the Use of Schools;* and in 1839 *A Manual of Useful Studies.* These works are not of great interest, since they often exhibit the cut-and-paste method of putting together a text. In his later years, however, Webster did publish a *History of the United States* that stands as an important document illustrating many of the beliefs that Webster held late in life.

Published originally in 1832, the book was revised and expanded slightly in 1835. In all, this work went through thirteen editions, the last in 1841. It did not receive a wide reading, no doubt reflecting Webster's growing alienation from the mainstream of American thought. The text, at first glance, appears to be a tedious narrative of American life up to the Constitution. Nevertheless, a closer reading reveals the profound influence of religion on Webster after his conversion in 1808. His own religious feelings and his response to political and social change pushed him away from the easygoing moralism of the 1780s toward a much harsher, more Calvinistic, and more outright religious worldview.

Webster's account of America's historical role was framed in religious terms. His retelling of the American past, for example, begins with Genesis and the dispersion of men. His basic goal was to show the close connection between American political development and the Christian religion. For example, he stated in the Preface that it was his "sincere desire" that Americans "should early understand that the genuine source of correct republican principles is the Bible, particularly the New Testament, or the christian [*sic*] religion."[13]

The linking of politics and religion was most vivid in his treatment of the Puritans. He wrote William C. Fowler that in his history of the United States "I have endeavored to honor our Puritan ancestors as the founders of the first genuine republics in the world and affirmed that the principles of republican government have their origin in the Scriptures."[14] Webster maintained that the Puritans were the most important source "for the progress and enjoyment of civil and religious liberty. . . ." Puritan republicanism was rooted in several factors, according to Webster. Their desire to organize each congregation independent of "ecclesiastical orders" was important to the growth of republican principles. Equally important was the policy of distributing land "in free hold" so that each citizen was "lord of his own soil" and economically able to defend his independence. Furthermore, the Puritans "founded governments on the principle that the people are the sources of power . . ." and they also established schools so that "all members of their communities . . . might learn their rights and duties." It is important to remember that, in Webster's view, the Puritans derived this plan solely from the Bible and the principles of true Christianity (*H*, 300–302).

The influence of the Puritans was most strongly felt in New England where it produced a people Webster clearly favored. For him, New Englanders "are remarkable for their industry, invention and perseverance. They make the most diligent farmers and mechanics; and the most active, bold and hardy seamen on earth. They are distinguished for their habits of subordination to parental and civil authority, which render them peaceable, obliging and hospitable . . ." (*H*, 320). He admitted that one could find a few corrupt souls in New England, but these unregenerate few are often those who do not own their own land and, most important, they are those who do not live "in the constant attendance upon religious worship. . . ." The true New Englander—a descendent of the Puritan—a land owner, a church-goer, a citizen—possessed the "habit of subordination" (*H*, 321).

Puritanism was not only responsible for the New England character, it was also crucial to the American Revolution. In 1832 Webster saw the Puritan influence as central in the revolt against England. The rudimentary republicanism of the Puritans had established the predisposition to rebel against the corrupt and arbitrary English government. After success in America, the republican tradition passed on to France, Greece, and Latin America. For Webster, rationalistic ideas and Enlightenment thinkers have magically disappeared. The American Revolution was, in no way, a product of radical European thought. The French thinkers that influenced him in the early 1780s find no place in his history. He made the facts fit his religious view of America's past—a past with no room for infidel Enlightenment thinkers.

In view of his highly religious view of the American Revolution, Webster had a problem dealing with Tom Paine, a noted infidel. Paine and his pamphlet *Common Sense* had played a central role in preparing Americans to accept the idea of independence. Webster, in 1832, was clearly uncomfortable in the presence of the memory of Paine. Portraying him as "an Englishman of low birth" who "possessed a popular talent at writing," Webster gave Paine his due for preparing the minds of the people for the idea of independence. Paine's role in the Revolution, however, came before "he debased himself by infidelity and licentious principles" (referring to Paine's anti-Christian writings from the 1790s), and he could not have had the impact he had without the support and aid of "eminent characters." In dealing with Paine, Webster struggled to play down the role of a man he saw as an apostle of the irreligion of the European Enlightenment (*H*, 240).

The treatment of Paine was only one example of Webster's religious orientation in an otherwise straightforward narrative. At the end of the text he abandoned history altogether and attached a section called "Advice to the Young." This nineteen-page testament is an important source for understanding Webster in his later years.

In the guise of offering useful advice to young people, Webster stated his position on basic social, political, and religious issues. Central to all these positions was an all-powerful God to whom men owed total submission. This was a much different God from the benign Being who appeared in Webster's work in the 1780s. The deity who slipped in and out of the speller and the reader was very much a god of reason. Men knew God existed because they were possessed of reason. In the *History of the United States* reason has given way to revelation. We do not know God by examining His works or by any other means except the Bible, a book in which God "has graciously revealed his character to man. . . ." It is from this same book that we learn what God wants from us. His first command is "to love the Lord your God with all the heart and soul and mind and strength." God sent to earth a Redeemer, Jesus Christ, whose life of perfect obedience to God's law men should imitate. Faith in Christ and a sincere attempt to follow his footsteps are the keys to immortality (*H*, 321–324). Webster believed that God commanded a second class of duties—those that we owe to our fellowmen. Basic to these was the Golden Rule. Yet Webster seemed more interested in instilling a proper deference to parents and superiors. God, according to Webster, wants "superiors" to be given perpetual honor and respect.

While his "Advice to the Young" was generally more religious than his earlier work, it did contain themes that first appeared in early texts. For example, he advised youth on the virtues of hard work. "Time" is God's gift to man to be used "for employment, not waste." He continued, "most men are obliged to labor for subsistence; and this is a happy arrangement of things by divine appointment; as labor is one of the best preservatives both of health and of moral habits. But if you are not under the necessity of laboring for subsistence, let your time be occupied which shall do good to your-

selves and your fellow men. Idleness tends to lead men into vicious
pleasures: and to waste time is to abuse the gifts of God" (*H,* 335).
Earlier, before his conversion, Webster had been a strong advocate of
hard work and the idea that wealth entailed responsibilities. Yet he
had never tied these concepts quite so tightly to God. In his later
years what had once been a moral maxim became a divine decree.

Webster touched on a number of other issues in the *History* that
indicate the influence of Christianity on his later thought. Women
were advised to know their station, support their men, and stay at
home; it was their Christian duty to do so. Voting was a right
fraught with grave religious implications; when a citizen cast a vote,
he was under God's injunction "to choose for rulers, *just men who will
rule in the fear of God."* This was crucial because "the preservation of
a republican government depends on the faithful discharge of this
duty" (*H,* 336). Literature, in the form of drama, novels, and tales,
may provide amusement but ultimately it corrupts its readers. "The
most perfect maxims" are in the Bible. The clergy, in his view, were
under attack in the 1830s and Webster came to their defense. The
clergy were the best supports of Christianity, and Christianity was
"the foundation of public order, of liberty and of republican
government."

His *History of the United States* gives us some idea of the change that
took place in Webster's thinking between the 1780s and the 1830s.
His basic positions remain much the same but they have taken a
deeply religious tone. Webster had always called for a virtuous,
thrifty, and hardworking population as the basis for the American republic. The political controversies and upheavals of the 1780s and
1790s had made him an anxious republican, one who sought firm authority in a period of great change. He found it in God.

Educational Theory

In the wake of the American Revolution many Americans believed
the time was ripe to reform many basic social institutions. Education
was no exception, and Webster was, during the 1780s, in the fore-
front of the movement to remodel America's schools. Early in his career he saw schools as a means of molding the typical child into a
moral, virtuous, and economically self-sufficient republican adult.
After the political storms of the 1790s Webster's views on education
changed. He still sought schools and education that would control
the passions of youth and turn young people into socially useful citi-

zens. His later views on education, however, gave religion a much greater role and his opinion of mankind had grown much darker. The 1790s were, for Webster, a dividing line; before their arrival he was full of hope, and his thought has a utopian thread in it. After 1800 hopefulness declined, and fear and anxiety grew. The child was no longer a blank slate capable of perfection but innately a sinner to be checked and controlled by a humbling religion and a demanding God. Perhaps nowhere else was this change more stark than in the two most important statements he made on education—one in 1790, the other in 1823.

"On the Education of Youth in America." This essay is basic to an understanding of Webster. It appeared originally in six installments in his *American Magazine,* and he included it in a collection of his essays published in 1790. Modern scholars have reprinted it and have often cited it as typical of Webster's thought. [15]

He began with two basic points: education shapes the individual and individuals shape the nation; and the type of education found in a society has always been molded to the particular circumstances of that society. Webster believed that simple societies sought education that would bring security; healthy, growing societies wanted "utility" from education while highly civilized cultures sought "show and amusement." Webster saw the United States in the middle of the process—a robust society in need of a practical educational system.

Education was for Webster "an object of great magnitude." It had an important and complex job to do; it must "implant in the minds of the American youth the principles of virtue and of liberty and inspire them with just and liberal ideas of government and with an inviolable attachment to their own country" (*Ed,* 45).

He turned from this general statement of purpose to what he considered the common errors America had to avoid in its schools. Americans have, in the first place, inherited "a too general attention to dead languages, with a neglect of our own." He defended the emphasis on English as utilitarian. Those few going on into learned professions should study Latin and Greek but for the average American dead languages were a waste of time. Webster noted that language study was unpopular because of dry and boring teaching methods and attacked the teaching of Latin before English grammar. A second error involved the use of the Bible as a schoolbook. Webster was against this practice because he felt familiarity bred contempt. The use of the Bible as a schoolbook was quite an issue during the 1780s. In the preface to his reader he had criticized the use of the

Bible and considerable criticism had been directed at him. Quietly he deleted this statement from the schoolbooks. His view of the Bible was conditioned by his involvement in the publishing of schoolbooks. He believed that children should learn to read and spell from books designed for the purpose. The Bible was a book for the home and church.

He was very much interested in teachers. Webster thought that the lack of good teachers was the "principal defect" in American schools. He was astonished that "parents wish their children to be *well-bred,* yet place them under the care of *clowns.*" In effect, Webster was asking that Americans pay more to get better teachers. Those in charge of schools were often forced to hire "clowns" and disreputable characters because they could afford no better. This practice, according to Webster, introduced children to vice and immorality through the example of their teachers. Laws and preaching would do little good once young people had been exposed to bad examples. Instruction by moral teachers was important because he believed that the only "practicable method to reform mankind is to begin with children, to banish . . . from their company every low-bred drunken immoral character." Webster's faith in the notion that a good environment would produce good character was unbounded in the 1780s. In this he was truly an Enlightenment thinker (*Ed,* 57–59).

After listing the errors he found in the present school systems, the essay suggested a positive program for schools in a republic. A successful republic must be based on two "regulations": land must be widely distributed so that every citizen shall have the "power of acquiring what his industry merits," and have the economic basis for political independence. A republic must also have a system of education that provides its people with "an opportunity of acquiring knowledge and fitting himself for places of trust." Both points have clear democratic implications. The schools had to be both good and readily available in order to prepare every citizen to function politically—as voter and officeholder. Webster attacked elite education that excluded the "poorer rank"; this was "monarchical," not republican education (*Ed,* 65–66).

While the essay demanded schooling for everyone, not everyone was to receive the same schooling. Women were destined for a somewhat different education. Webster saw "the ladies" as filling a special role in society: they raised and educated children and were largely responsible for "controlling the manners of a nation." Their training should fit this special role; it should include reading and writing (no French), arithmetic, geography, poetry, and drawing and dance for young ladies in large towns. The ladies should not read novels. Education should prepare women to occupy a special place: "In all nations a *good* education is that which renders ladies correct in their manners, respectable in their families, and agreeable in society. That education is always *wrong* which raises a woman above the duties of her station" (*Ed,* 70).

The essay also contained a general condemnation of Europe. Specifically, Webster argued that the United States had no reason to emulate the European educational system. The American republic would be foolhardy if it developed "a taste for copying the luxurious manners and amusements of England and France." As a first step, America should stop recruiting teachers in Europe and families should stop sending boys abroad for their education. European ideas such as monarchy tended to come with European instructors, and a foreign education attached one to a foreign nation rather than to one's homeland. At the same time, Webster suggested that "a liberal education" should include a tour of the United States, not Europe.

The essay ended with a plea: "Americans, unshackle your minds and act like independent beings. You have been children long enough . . ." (*Ed,* 77). This advice reflected Webster's major goal in the essay; he wanted Americans to free themselves from European models in order to create schools that would serve a republic. His demand was, in turn, bolstered by the notion that each generation was a blank slate upon which the schools could write. "On the Education of Youth in America" was an intensely optimistic essay in which Webster foresaw the schools molding a generation of independent and virtuous republicans, devoted to their country and possessed of an education specially modeled to their needs.

"Letter to a Young Gentleman . . ." This essay was published originally in 1823 and included in Webster's final collection of essays in 1843. Webster's views had changed so dramatically that they are difficult to compare with his earlier position. Education was defined in very different terms. Gone completely was his emphasis on nationalism, his distrust of Europe, and the separation of the Bible from schooling. Yet, at the same time, there were links to the earlier view. Webster was still a utilitarian, but he had clearly redefined "utility." Education should still meet needs but by 1823 the needs had changed.

Webster began the essay with a confession. He was eager to direct the course of a young man's education, since "no small portion of my life has been spent in correcting the errors of my early education."[16] The remainder of the work was a list of these corrections.

The first injunction to the young man was to be deferential. The young should be guided by the old until they reach a level of wisdom and experience that will allow them to join the discourse over issues as equals. The earlier essay on education was marked by an eagerness to reject the old patterns and it urged America to set off in new directions. In the thirty-plus years between these works Webster had acquired a deep reverence for tradition and the idea of deference to elders with more wisdom and experience.

He goes on to counsel the young man to begin his education by first asking certain questions. *"Who made me? Why was I made? What is my duty?* The proper answers to these questions, and the practical results, constitute, my dear friend, the whole business of life." The student should use reason to find answers to these questions, "but reason, without cultivation, without experience and without the aid of revelation is a miserable guide. . . ." The best source from which to learn about the creator is the Bible. Likewise, the Bible is also central because everything—happiness, tranquillity, reputation— "depend on an exact conformity of conduct to the commands of God revealed in the sacred oracles." These commands often direct youth to honor age and their parents: "The command to honor your father and mother comprehends not only due respect and obedience to our parents; but all due respect to other superiors. . . . The distinction of age is one established by God himself and is perhaps the only difference of rank in society, which is of divine origin" (*Co,* 297).

A young man must choose his reading, beyond the Bible, with great care. Only those works that improve "morals, literature, arts and science; preferring profit to pleasure, and instruction to amusement" were truly useful. A good education allotted "a small portion of time" to light reading that "tends to relax the mind," but the great part "is to be employed in useful labors. . . ." This relationship between amusement and utility is crucial because a student "hurried along with the current of popular reading" risked not only his time but also eventual "imbecility." Grave danger lurked in the theater, almost all plays "contained sentiments which are offensive to moral purity." Webster's utilitarian philosophy also weighed against drama:

"Before I can believe the stage to be a school of virtue, I must demand proof that a single profligate has ever been reformed, or a single man or woman made a Christian by its influence" (*Co, 300*).

The last part of the essay has little to do with education. Instead, Webster offered to the young man advice on proper political philosophy. A republic was a fragile form of government, Webster claimed, and its citizens must hold certain views if republicanism was to survive. They must hold the old and wise in deferential awe; they must vote only for Christian gentlemen *"who rule in the fear of God"*; they must never join secret organizations, and finally they should constantly be on the watch for "corruption."

"Letter to a Young Gentleman" illustrated both the degree to which Webster had changed and the degree to which he had remained the same. Education was still a very practical matter but his goals had been greatly altered. In the late 1780s he saw education creating a responsible citizenry able to vote and even hold office intelligently. They would be full of virtue, but this virtue had only minor religious elements. Schools were a crucial issue in 1790; they would be the means of shaping the people to assume their republican responsibilities. By 1823 Webster cared little about schools per se; this essay does not mention them at all. Instead, he sought a practical education to mold a people deferential to their elders and responsive to God and His laws. The Bible has become the starting point and guiding light of true learning. Implicit in both essays was a fear of "corruption" and its tendency to lead the people astray. Fiction and drama should be shunned, the people must be made upright and moral. In 1790 Webster believed schools were the answer; in 1823 they had been replaced by God.

Thus, for Webster, education was always an instrument used to accomplish some social or political purpose; learning was never, for him, an endeavor with intrinsic worth. In this he reflected the times; in the 1780s American revolutionaries had quickly seized upon education as a device to help create the self-sacrificing and virtuous citizenry that they thought necessary for a stable republic, and, likewise, after 1800 those caught up in the religious revivals sought to use education to further their religious goals. Ironically, this process helped make America a bustling marketplace selling countless varieties of education. Legions of special interest groups with their own political, social, and religious aims established schools and promoted their own educational theories to secure their goals. Webster, for example, was a member of the group who founded Amherst College with the idea that it would further the cause of orthodox Calvinist beliefs in a nation they saw as overrun by religious liberalism. As Lawrence Cremin has concluded, the result of these educational developments was to move American education "in the direction of increased diversity and choice." So many groups attempted to arrest or further change that "the greater availability of diverse options that resulted from their efforts, extended the choice for individuals . . ." and this "afforded people the possibility of release from geographical and social place, and in so doing augmented personal liberty."[17]

After 1830, Webster, in his personal correspondence, indicated that he was aware of this situation. The classroom and the library, he thought, had become too much like a battlefield. In a letter to William Chauncey Fowler he confessed that the addition of books to libraries made him apprehensive because the introduction of new books "will produce rivalships or competition which may disturb our districts." The committees that select the books can hardly do so "without giving offense . . ." or "bringing into the libraries party productions and sectarian views that produce unpleasant collisions." In another letter to Fowler, Webster complained that "our citizens are too much disposed to *multiply* seminaries of learning rather than *improve* the course of studies in those which now exist."[18] Both letters convey the impression that Webster saw American education as chaotic and potentially destructive and that, if he could, he would reduce education to a system that passed on only one political persuasion and one morality.

He never realized that he was a small part of the problem. He never understood that his wishes for American education were just as partisan as those of the next man. Webster, for example, wrote Solomon Smead that "I should rejoice to see a system adopted that should lay a foundation for a permanent fund for public schools. . . ." This was, however, not part of some democratic dream; Webster wanted well-supported public schools so as "to have more pains taken to discipline our youth in early life in sound maxims of moral, political, and religious duties. I believe more than is commonly believed may be done in this way towards correcting the vices and disorders of society."[19]

Furthermore, Webster disliked the idea that education should lead to social mobility. For "the yeomanry of our country" he wanted schooling "proper to make them *intelligent and useful* in the spheres which they are to occupy." He believed that all the experiments in education he saw around him

will encourage the indisposition to labor and foster the disrelish or contempt of it which now manifest themselves in all parts of our country. All young persons seem desirous to *get above* manual labor and be gentlemen, whether they have property or not, or, at least, to seek a living in some occupation more genteel than farming and mechanical employment.[20]

Webster wrote this in 1837; more than sixty years earlier a Connecticut farm boy, in love with books, sought a local preacher who could teach him Greek and Latin, and the young lad trained for college. Off he went to Yale saying good-bye to farm labor; he was eager to make his living by writing words, not by plowing fields. The youth became well known in America, he wrote a spelling book that for millions served as the first step away from the farm or the shop. He became genteel, and when he was nearly eighty he wanted to close the road that he had taken from a rocky New England farm to that gentility. Time clouds even the best minds.

There is one final irony. While Webster's later opinions about education were colored by his conservatism and his religious feelings, his most fundamental contributions had come earlier and they had helped drive American education away from religion and toward secularity. The early schoolbooks and his essay "On the Education of Youth in America" had de-emphasized religious instruction and had conceptualized education as primarily practical and political. In comparison to colonial schoolbooks his works were hardly religious at all. They carried forward the moralism and emphasis on virtue of *The New England Primer,* but they sharply reduced the role of God in the lives of American youth. His emphasis on the practical and political uses of education, in the long run, was infinitely more important than his later religious approach to educational issues.

Chapter Three
Politics

In May 1843 Noah Webster summarized the course of his political thought that had taken him from youthful revolutionary enthusiasm to the despair of his old age:

To a man who has witnessed the noble principles of the revolutionary republicans—who elected men to office solely for their sound wisdom, eminent and tried patriotism—how afflicting, how depressing must be the changes which have taken place, since we see the great talents of the country neglected, and weak, visionary or profligate men purchasing offices by servility to parties and party-men! What hope can be now entertained of preserving our republican institutions![1]

This journey involved several important changes of mind; of which the most important was Webster's gradual loss of faith in the people's ability to govern themselves, in their virtue, and in their ability to subordinate individual interests to the common good. As a young man he believed that the people, if educated and given property, could be the basis of a stable and virtuous republic. As he grew older he lost this faith; Americans elected weak and profligate men and showed themselves prone to the flattery of "parties and party-men." He was appalled by the growing lack of deference shown by the people to "the great talents of the country." If men of experience and age who understood the public interest could not gain the trust and votes of the people, then Americans must be checked by some other force.

What caused Webster to change his political views so dramatically? In large part, events pushed him toward a more conservative position. The Middletown Convention in 1783 was probably the first event to shake his faith in the people, but it was only part of a general crisis of authority that shook the United States in the 1780s and 1790s. The French Revolution and the disruptions it caused in the United States were crucial in finally undermining Webster's optimistic revolutionary faith. Jefferson's election in 1800 was important because of the new president's religious and political views, but Webster was also profoundly frightened by the clamor and hostility of the campaign. Leadership was not something two parties struggled for; it was, for Webster, handed calmly by the people to the wisest and more experienced. To some extent, events merely pushed to the fore Webster's conservative New England biases. An habitual deference to, and the assumption of, Christian humility in leaders were deeply engrained in him, and these inclinations slowly rose to the surface as he grew older. Finally, we have to understand that Webster worked incredibly hard to carve a niche among a certain elite. His friends and associates were almost entirely New England Federalists, and Webster's sense of status and importance was, in large part, bound up with the success or failure of this group. When the Federalist control of the national government was challenged in the 1790s, Webster felt his own status threatened. Unlike political parties in later American history, the Federalists of the 1790s had no room in their political universe for persistent conflict between parties. To the end of his life Webster refused to accept party conflict and railed against the disruptive nature of what he liked to call factions.

Almost everything Webster wrote had a political element in it. His schoolbooks, for example, were intended to educate children, but they were also political tracts designed to create a certain political attitude. As a journalist, politics was never far from his mind. Even his dictionaries were political. They were motivated by feelings of nationalism and a desire to use language as a device to create a stable republic. In this chapter, however, we shall look only at those documents that were solely political in nature.

Early Views

In Webster's scattered early political writings we find a young revolutionary with strong utopian and ascetic tendencies. While teaching in Sharon, Connecticut, in 1782, Webster wrote three essays that appeared in the *New York Packet*. Later he added three additional essays, publishing the six pieces in the *Freeman's Chronicle* in 1783 under the title "Observations on the Revolution of America." These essays were written by a young man who had found in the American Revolution the hope of mankind. He invited "the good and the brave of all nations . . . to the last resort of liberty and religion." America was going to be "the closing scene of a vast drama" in which "vice and despotism will be shrouded in despair, and virtue and freedom triumph in the rewards of peace, security and happiness."[2]

Great Britain, Webster claimed, had forced America to play this heroic role. Webster put the revolutionary conflict in family terms. The colonies had been the dutiful children of England, but they had been "driven by necessity to abandon the parent state." America was "fond of her new situation," and there was as little chance that she would "revert back to a state of dependence, as a bride to quit the partner of her heart, for the company of sullen age. . . ."[3] It seems likely that Webster's view of the relations between America and Great Britain was colored by his own separation from his father. As a young well-educated man testing his own independence, he could easily see his country doing the same.

He believed that Americans were innately virtuous and that liberty would be safe in their hands. He had no fear that the people would abuse their new rights because "the people will never make laws oppressive to themselves." Webster was a strong advocate of frequent elections because "where annual elections end tyranny begins."[4] At the base of all these views was a total faith in the people and their virtue, but as time passed Webster lost his faith.

The tone of these early essays was more important than their content. Webster, in the early 1780s, never doubted that the oppressed colonies, when freed from England, could thrive and become a showplace for the rest of the world. He noted that some European critics had predicted that America would soon turn to luxury and dissipation and that contacts with the French (their ally in the Revolution) would hinder the Protestant religion and introduce popery. Webster called these prophecies "phantoms" and "mere illusions." "The kingdoms of Europe" were the very fountain of human discord and, according to Webster, America was free of the problems that beset the Old World and was setting out to create a society free of "wrangling sectaries." The new American nation would rest

upon the idea of an universal toleration: she admits all religions into her bosom—she secures the sacred rights of every individual: and (astonishing absurdity to Europeans!) she sees a thousand discordant opinions live in the strictest harmony of friendship. This priviledge of an unprecedented toleration must incite nations into her dominions; preserve a tranquility in society that must cast a shade upon all the Hierarchies of the earth—it will finally raise her to a pitch of greatness and lustre, before which the glory of Greece and Rome shall dwindle to a point, and the splendor of modern Empires shall fade into obscurity.[5]

Thus, Webster at twenty-five had caught the contagion of a revolutionary age. His faith knew no bounds; America would become the virtuous counterpoint to corrupt Europe, and oppressed mankind would flood New World shores seeking liberty and toleration. These essays were charged with an emotionalism that was common at the time. Few Americans, Webster included, could foresee the problems that lay in the future. "Universal toleration" would prove to be a thorny basis upon which to rest a nation. Slowly, he realized that "a thousand discordant opinions" could not "live in the strictest harmony."

Sketches of American Policy

After returning to Hartford in 1783 from Goshen, New York, Webster attempted to practice law. Since cases were few and far between, he had time to write and he used it to good advantage. In the nearly three years ending in the spring of 1785 he wrote the three parts of his *Grammatical Institute* and his most substantial essay on politics, *Sketches of American Policy* (1785). The essay first appeared as a pamphlet and Webster distributed copies of it during his travels in 1785–1786. It met with some success and parts, or all of it, appeared in a number of newspapers. The work was divided into four parts. The first section contained Webster's theory of government; the second was a discussion of European governments; the third contrasted American governments with European, and the fourth was a plan for improving the American system.

The first section, "Theory of Government," echoed much that appeared in "Observations on the Revolution of America." Webster, inspired by his reading of Rousseau, claimed that the state originated in a social contract and the purpose of the contract was to protect the natural rights of the weak against the strong. Such a state could not become oppressive because the people will not pass laws that oppress them and "the essence of sovereignty consists in the general voice of the people." In any sizable state the people must elect representatives to act for them, but such surrogates must remain "servants" to the people. While Webster was interested in governments that served the people, he was also interested in efficient governments that could act with authority. His perfect government, therefore, was one "where the right of *making* laws is vested in the greatest number of individuals . . ." and "the power of *executing* them in the smallest number."[6]

In the second section, "Governments on the Eastern Continent," Webster drew a number of lessons from European political experience. He acknowledged that Europe has some good rulers and excellent legal systems but no sound constitutions. Nowhere in Europe did he find the essential ingredient for a truly free government: "an equal distribution of property." For him, most civil discord arose from the inequitable distribution of property, but this theory was not as radical as it sounded because he clearly indicated that he desired only a roughly equal distribution of wealth; his main fear was a system of holding property "to which are annexed certain hereditary offices and dignities." Europeans were also hampered in their attempts to create free governments by "the establishment or preference, given to some religious persuasion." He concluded that because of unequal property-holding and religious establishments most Europeans "are mostly chained in vassalage—without knowledge, without freedom and without hope of relief." He suggested that there was little hope for Europe beyond "gradual alterations" (*Sk*, 18–20).

In the third section he compared oppressed Europe with enlightened America. While European systems of government were "laid by barbarians, in whom the military spirit was high," the American government was "framed in the most enlightened period of the world." Webster praised several post-revolutionary developments that would help ensure American freedom. He lauded, for example, the end of primogeniture and entail and the confiscation and division of large estates as measures that would further increase the number of property owners.

As a true son of New England, he saw the American South as a problem, but he was optimistic that this would change. The South contained too much of the "aristocratic genius of European governments," but Webster believed that the South would inevitably be republican. He thought that the slave trade would end, thus dooming the plantation system and the aristocratic class it supported. The South also failed to educate its citizens, a crucial necessity in a republic. New England, on the other hand, largely without slaves and with a historic commitment to education, was Webster's model, and he implied that the rest of the nation should look to the New England states for true republican principles (*Sk*, 23–25).

The last section began with a question: what can cause a bond to exist among the states? Webster rejected a standing army, religion, and the threat of external force. Rather than any of these, Webster suggested "a supreme power at the head of the union . . ." to unite the states and overcome minority opposition to just and necessary measures. If such a supreme power was not created, Webster predicted disaster. He believed that a monarchy would soon be erected on the ruins of republican civil dissensions and to prevent this he urged "a supreme power over the whole, with authority to compel obedience to legal measures . . ." (*Sk,* 31, 43).

The *Sketches* was not great political thought, but it clearly illustrated Webster's response to the times. By the mid-1780s, Webster was a fragile combination of fear and optimism. In the first three sections the radicalism and utopianism of the early eighties dominated, but in the last section fears of chaos and instability, perhaps rooted most centrally in his response to the Middletown Convention, took center stage. Near the end of the fourth section he listed the three characteristics he most wanted the American republic to possess: "a general diffusion of knowledge, an encouragement of industry, frugality and virtue; and a sovereign power at the head of the states" (*Sk,* 48). Here was the position of a man seeking control, order, authority; and, for the rest of his life, education in one form or the other, frugality, virtue, and a powerful executive would be fundamental aspects of his thought.

In the very last paragraph of the *Sketches* Webster revealed his most basic concern in the mid-1780s—it may have been the most basic concern in all his writings. Education, virtue, and a powerful executive must do battle with the fragmentation of interests. Americans should employ these tools to bring countless local and individual interests into line and subordinate them to the public good. Webster believed that "we cannot and ought not wholly to divest ourselves of provincial views and attachments, but we should subordinate them to the general interests of the continent." Every American, Webster asserted, had a number of "obligations"; his family, his business, and his state all had interests that deserved protection. However, "as a citizen and subject of the American empire, he had a national interest far superior to all others. Every relation in society constitutes some obligations, which are proportional to the magnitude of the society." Webster did not simply ask for the sacrifice of self-interest to that of the nation. For him, there was no sacrifice involved. In fact, he claimed that "self interest, both in morals and in politics, is and ought to be the ruling principle of mankind; but this principle must operate in perfect conformity to social and political obligations." What was best for the nation was ultimately best for the individual. Webster had faith that "but a few years experience will correct our ideas of self interest," and that Americans would soon understand "that *provincial interest* is inseparable from *national interest.*"

There was nothing really new about these principles; any literate American Puritan in 1640 would have agreed with them. Indeed, Webster's opinions on the relationship between interests were slightly reactionary in 1785. His ideal republic in which all interests were subjugated to a general national interest required a social and intellectual uniformity that did not exist in America. Sectional and class interests had become an important reality in American life in the eighteenth century. America was quickly becoming a complex society in which large farmers and small farmers had conflicting values. Seacoast commercial interests fought against a powerful agrarian lobby and the slave-owner eyed the non-slave-owner with suspicion. Such realities were rapidly pushing American politics toward a system that sought to compromise and mute conflicting claims. The vision of society as an organic whole was retreating in the face of a newer vision that accepted the reality of plural and unreconcilable interests. Webster's conception of an organic community with a single dominating purpose was a legacy of the New England past where simple villages and colonies animated by religious purpose and a sense of collective tradition were capable of establishing agreement on the nature of the general interest. In those simple communities the idea of endless political conflict over public policy was abhorrent; disruptive individuals like Roger Williams were given ample opportunity to accept the community's general purpose and were banished when they refused. America, in 1785, was a much more complex society. Indeed, within two decades, organized political factions would become a fixture on the political landscape, and with them would come the gradual acceptance of perpetual political conflict between groups. Webster would never totally accept this change. He would cling to the idea that any society had to have a single dominating interest to which all others must pay homage.

As time passed, Webster rejected the positions he had taken in the first three parts of the *Sketches,* but remained proud of the fourth. By the late 1790s he was beginning to regret some of what he had written in the 1785 pamphlet. He wrote Jedidiah Morse in July 1797 that the *Sketches* were "a little too democratic for my present notions. I was once a visionary and should now leave out a few views contained in it. It contains also a few remarks on the Southern States which I should suppress. On the whole however, I agree with myself in 1785." In marginal notes apparently written by Webster in his own copy of the *Sketches* at different times he withdrew even more clearly from his original position. In one such note, for example, he wrote that "the three first Sketches contain many . . . notions . . . which can never be reduced to practice" and "shortsighted as I was; I did not foresee the force of party."[7] In retrospect, the *Sketches* were written by a man in the process of change from an earlier, more radical political position to one that called for more control and order.

In 1787 Webster wrote a short piece that should be considered together with *Sketches of American Policy*. After the Constitution was drafted, it quickly attracted both defenders and opponents. Webster was one of the first to rush to the new Constitution's defense with the publication of *An Examination into the Leading Principles of the Federal Constitution*. . . . It was, by Webster's own admission, "a hasty production" written at the request of Thomas Fitzsimmons, a Pennsylvania delegate to the Constitutional Convention.

In large part, the pamphlet was devoted to answering objections to the new Constitution. First of all, he defended the bicameral legislature as necessary to check the passions that too easily erupted in a single-chamber legislative body. Next, he rejected the idea that giving each state two senators amounted to unequal representation. Senators, he felt, would speak for "the whole confederacy" and not limited special interests. In any event, the House of Representatives was "the more immediate voice of the separate states,"[8] and the Senate was designed as a check on the democratic nature of the House.

In general, he promoted the document as the device that would ensure American liberty and a glowing American future. Without some strong federal authority the United States can have "no union, no respectability, no national character . . . no national justice. . . ." He still believed that liberty stood "on the unmoveable basis of a general distribution of property and the diffusion of knowledge," but Americans "must cease to contend, to fear, and to hate, before they can realize the benefits of independence and government or enjoy the blessings, which heaven has lavished in rich profusion upon this western world" (55).

The Constitution was an important document in Webster's life. His *Sketches* had been one of the first publications to call for a federal system to control the states and his defense of the Constitution in 1787 had helped obtain ratification. More important, however, the Constitution seemed to restore his faith and optimism about the American republic. The Constitution, with its intricate set of checks and balances and its limitations on the direct influence of the people, calmed his fears of popular disorders and eternal contention between factions. Webster had faith that the Senate and the President were safely insulated against the passions of the people. He believed that the federal Constitution reflected "the wisdom of all ages collected. . . . In short, it is an *empire of reason*" (6).

Giles Hickory

During the year that Webster was editor of the *American Magazine,* he wrote a series of essays on politics using the pseudonym Giles Hickory. These pieces were rambling and hastily written, but they also clearly identified the most fundamental conflicts of the late 1780s. Some opponents of the Constitution demanded a bill of rights and other constitutional devices that would make the fundamental frame of government unalterable by the legislature. Webster saw republican government in a much different way than did these antifederalists. At the core of his criticism of the antifederalists was Webster's belief that sovereignty must rest with the elected representatives of the people, not the people themselves. In this he was responding to a decade of political turmoil in which legislatures at the state and national level had been hamstrung by the constant interference of the people in their deliberations. Special conventions (such as the Middletown affair in Connecticut) and the practice of giving local instructions to representatives had played havoc with the efficient operation of government. For these reasons Webster advocated, in the *Sketches,* a supreme head of government removed from local interests and thus able to make and administer law efficiently. As Giles Hickory, he argued against a bill of rights and an unalterable constitution as inefficient and unnecessary.

A device such as a bill of rights assumed that the people's liberty could be guaranteed in an unalterable constitution. Webster, on the other hand, believed that "liberty is never secured by such paper declarations; nor lost for want of them." He contended that government was essentially organic, taking its form from "the genius and habits of the people." Furthermore, the nature of government would and should change as "the temper of the people" changed. Any list of rights or any written constitution should not, and could not, be unalterable since the force of changing habits and needs would be irresistible. In demanding such unalterable forms Americans had, in Webster's view, relied too heavily on European experience. European governments had always invested an individual or a political body with rights and powers "independent of the suffrages of the body of the subjects. A Bill of Rights against the encroachments of Kings and Barons, or against any power independent of the people, is perfectly intelligible; but a Bill of Rights against the encroachments of an elective legislature, that is, against our *own* encroachments on ourselves, is a curiosity in government."[9]

Webster was baffled by the people's fear that an elected government was a threat to their rights and liberty. Such a fear must be "directed *against themselves,* or against an invasion which they *imagine* may happen in future ages" (75). He pointed out that the present age had no right to make laws for those not yet born—a point often made by proponents of a bill of rights, such as Jefferson. Webster also wondered why the antifederalists had such faith in present legislatures and special conventions and so little in future ones. Unhampered by unalterable measures, bodies meeting in the future could and should adjust the laws to meet unforeseen developments. Furthermore, Webster asked, what was the difference between the regular legislature and a specially elected convention? They were both elected by the people and often contained the same men.

At the root of all these inconsistencies, Webster insisted, lay a fundamental misunderstanding about the nature of representation—revealed most clearly in the attempts by local constituencies to instruct their representatives. For Webster, this practice rested on the notion that the people in general, armed with little information and aware only of local interests, were the best judges of the appropriateness of a law. Webster would rather allow "the most judicious men . . . (for such generally are the Representatives)" to make such judgments because they possess "the best information from every quarter" and they are privy to "a full discussion of the subject in an assembly, where clashing interests conspire to detect error and suggest improvements." Thus, although the people commonly saw their representatives as their particular agents, Webster argued that a representative

who attended only to local interests "abuses his trust." To him much
of the turmoil of the 1780s was based in just this tyranny of local
interests over the general good (205).

Therefore, a major concern of the Giles Hickory essays was to establish the proper relationship between the people and the legislature. His position was grounded on the idea that *"the Legislature has
all the power, of all the people"* and that the state can contain no power
greater than the elected legislature. This was a compelling position,
but it was just as compelling when the British used it against the
Americans in the late 1760s and early 1770s. By 1788–1789 Webster's political position had come to include what had been a basic
premise of political theory in the eighteenth century: men in every
state must be subject to a supreme, absolute power. As he stated,
there could be "no power residing in the State at large, which does
not reside in the legislature." His ideas, while conventional in the
eighteenth century, were in direct conflict with the drift of political
thinking in America since 1776. As one Connecticut town expressed
itself in 1783, "there is an original, underived and incommunicable
authority and supremacy, in the collective body of the people, to
whom all delegated power must submit. . . ."[10] To men like Webster this absurd notion could only lead to disorder and inefficiency. In
the long run, the notion that the people were absolutely sovereign
would develop legal and historic reality through the growth of popular participation in politics and the constant appeals of public figures
to the people. As that happened, between 1790 and 1840, Webster,
predictably, was appalled.

It is probably fair to conclude that his stance in the Giles Hickory
essays was based on an honest consideration of the issues in America
and his immersion in British legal thinking. However, it is also fair
to suggest that Webster's position was based on at least one unac-
knowledged assumption and that his views were contradictory. Lurk-
ing between the lines of the Hickory essays was the assumption of a
deferential electorate. He had great faith that legislatures would inevitably contain only those men from the substantial classes and men
with wider experience and greater education than the people-at-large.
This kind of representative would be especially common in the federal
Congress, since the units of representation were so much larger. In
the case of the federal Senate elite legislators would be the rule because the people's will would be filtered by the state legislatures who
elected senators. In short, Webster would have put absolute sover-

eignty in the hands of the legislature rather than with the people because he reasoned that the deferential habits of the people would elect men who were more rational and less inclined to passionate flights than the people themselves.

Webster's views were contradictory because they were a mixture of absolutes and relative propositions. He believed absolutely that the legislature in a state should be sovereign; the idea of divided or mixed sovereignty appeared preposterous to him. On the other hand, he defined government and the people as evolving organic things, subject to change. By 1789 political theorists generally were forced to deal with profound historical transformations that had washed away many of the absolute notions of past ages. Both Webster and his foes, the antifederalists, took positions that sought to salvage absolute values in a world growing increasingly relative. Thus, it is not surprising that we should find such contradictions in Webster's political thinking. Jefferson, after all, declared that the dead should not exercise a tyranny over the living, while at the same time calling for an unalterable bill of rights.

Such contradictions and inconsistencies were the product of an intensely confusing and anxious period in American history. Beginning even before the war for independence was over and extending well into the 1780s, the newly freed colonies experienced what many commentators at the time thought was a profound crisis. A full understanding of the *Sketches,* the *Defense,* and the "Giles Hickory" essays requires an understanding of that crisis.

The years just prior to the outbreak of the war and the conflict itself had been intensely ideological. Drawing on a number of sources for a political explanation of their revolution, Americans found particular force in the bundle of ideas often referred to as republican theory. At the heart of this theory was the belief that power was aggressive, always seeking as its victim the liberties of the people. Thus, British officialdom became for American revolutionaries the evil agent in the conflict. Americans saw themselves as victims of ambitious and corrupt men who sought to progressively deprive the colonies of their English liberties. The resistance to English measures and the decision to revolt were based, in large part, on this view of the relationship between power and liberty. How, then, did a state preserve liberty against corruption? The answer was to put the states in the hands of a government elected by a virtuous and vigilant people. They would elect only men of merit and talent and would prevent corruption, favoritism, and birth from becoming avenues to officeholding and power. Such a republican system, of course, required a special type of people and Webster defined them as well as anyone. Equal property-holding was essential; the landless urban rabble of Europe could not sustain a republican form of government. Also the people had to be educated so that they might responsibly exercise their new duties. The American Revolution thus aimed at nothing short of a utopian dream—a state governed by legislatures elected by a people virtuous, patriotic, and wise. The feeling that America was trying an awesome and novel experiment was common and, furthermore, the whole world, laden with monarchy, tyranny, and oppression, was watching the American republic and waiting for the first signs of failure.

They were not long in coming. By the early 1780s many Americans felt that the experiment was on the verge of failure. Furthermore, the problem causing the crisis came from an unexpected source. Common political wisdom held that power abused led to tyranny and that liberty abused led to anarchy. One would then expect the republican governments of the new United States to suffer from a lack of vigor and that government might even begin to crumble. Instead, America seemed to be suffering from an excess of government, from too many laws, not too few. The popularly elected legislatures in the states legislated too much; they transgressed what thoughtful observers called the eternal principles of social justice. The sanctity of contracts, a stable currency, and consistent administration of justice seemed impossible in a state where the legislature changed the body of law every time they were petitioned by a group of citizens. When duly passed measures displeased the people, they pressured for their repeal before the ink was dry, and they failed to vote taxes to support the national government. Unpopular laws also spawned special "legislatures," such as the Middletown Convention, to force the alteration of legal measures. Perhaps more ominously, in a number of states, the legislature began to swallow up executive and judicial functions of government, leaving governors and judges almost powerless. The Americans, like Webster, who advocated the federal Constitution did so, in large measure, because they felt that the states suffered under a legislative tyranny and that this would eventually change the republican dream into a nightmare. Webster, for example, predicted that, without the Constitution, monarchy would soon be erected upon the ruins of republicanism.

Webster, and most of those like him, did not reject the popularly elected legislature as a crucial part of the American state. As we have seen, he continued to believe that the American people should share in government by voting in the legislature of their choice on election day. What he wanted was a deliberative body free to consider the questions that came before it unhindered by the constant influence of the people. Once these questions had been resolved and laws passed, they deserved a fair trial and efficient and just administration; only an executive removed from the popular tumult could accomplish this. The concept of a president insulated from the pressures that subverted the state legislatures conformed to Webster's plea for "a supreme power over the whole, with authority to compel obedience to legal measures. . . ." To some extent, this symbolized a lessening of the general fear of arbitrary power that had been a legacy of the Revolution; many Americans came to realize that government needed power to run the state—nearly a decade of government by legislature had proven that.

Thus, Webster wrote his political essays of the 1780s in the general context of a crisis of authority. The sanguine expectations about the character of the people had turned out to be too utopian and visionary. The people could not have such a direct voice in the workings of government; they could block just measures at the state level and cripple the workings of the national government. Given control of the state legislatures, they had turned them into monsters characterized by bickering factions, an excess of law, and a disregard for the national welfare. Men such as Webster, Madison, Hamilton, Washington, and many others (some like Madison would later part company with Webster) thought the process of government itself was threatened. The passage of a federal Constitution to control the states, a Constitution with extensive checks on the people's influence, was an important moment in Webster's life. He felt that the new national government would save the republic from ruin and disgrace before the world. He underestimated, however, the extent to which the people had become accustomed to their enlarged political role. In a decade the presidency would become the prize in a bitter party conflict. In less than five years measures of the new federal government would produce vicious debate and mobs in the streets. National politics, in short, would soon conform, in large part, to the same democratic impulses and equalitarian spirit that disrupted the state leg-

islatures. When Webster saw all this, his faith in political solutions
was shaken and slowly he began to turn to religion as a check on an
unruly people.

The Revolution in France . . .

The French Revolution, as it became more radical and violent,
forced Webster to clarify his political stance, and in the process of
clarifying his views he grew increasingly anxious about political, social, and religious developments. The best evidence of this increased
anxiety was his 1794 essay *The Revolution in France. . . .* On the surface, the essay (published as a pamphlet) seems a calm consideration
of the impact and future consequences of revolution in France, but a
deeper reading reveals Webster's growing concern about the changes
taking place in American life.

He had heartily approved of the early stages of the French revolt,
but as it grew more radical, and this radicalism began to spread to
other European nations and to the United States, he became alarmed.
The pamphlet is divided into sections: Introduction, Jacobin Society,
Commissioners, National Treasury, Probable Event (i.e., outcome) of
the War, Debts, Agriculture, Manufactures, Commerce, Arts and
Science, Religion, Morality, Government, Remarks, Application,
Appendix, and Conclusion. Webster intended, by this method, to
give a detailed and useful account of the state of affairs in France. In
much of the essay he simply outlined the course of events in France.
For example, he noted that the Jacobin Society had largely swept
away all opposition and that their success in the conflict with the allied monarchies was based on the "unprecedented union of the people
of France." Webster predicted that the change from a feudal land-
holding system to freehold would stimulate agricultural production.
Because old feudal traditions had also inhibited manufacturing, he
saw France making great strides in this area as well.[11]

Webster, however, gradually slipped from this stance as objective
reporter. Particularly in the sections on Religion, Morality, and Government, he betrayed his deep concern and his subjective response to
the news from France. The early revolutionary attack on Catholicism
was, for Webster, easily understood, but the assault on religion had
clearly gotten out of hand. "A race of literary men" dominated by
Voltaire and Rousseau had attempted to destroy all religion "and to
erect upon its ruins, the throne of reason." They had not simply sub-

stituted "deism" for Christianity; they had instead embraced "atheism and materialism." Webster saw this experimentalism as the product of "enthusiasm" and insisted that the new religious philosophy in France was based on superstition and passion—just as the dethroned tenets of Catholicism had been. Both philosophies were versions of idolatry—"once France idolized the priest and the Virgin, it now idolizes the enthroned Reason" (*Co*, 10–11).

Webster wanted to show that France was merely substituting one set of idols for another. He was disturbed by the veneration of liberty caps, for example, but nothing upset him more than the French legislation concerning names that, for example, banished Mr. and Mrs. and replaced them with the title "Citizen." He thought it natural that aristocratic distinctions should be eliminated but that "common titles of mere *civility* and *respect* should be attacked was astonishing. . . ." The French attack on such titles and their creation of a new calendar pushed him to one of his most emotional statements:

Such perpetual contradictions, such a series of puerile innovations are without parallel in the history of revolutions: and while these regenerators of a great nation believe themselves the devotees of *reason* and *philosophy,* and exult in their supereminent attainments, they appear to the surrounding world of indifferent spectators, as weak, as blind and as fanatical, as a caravan of Mohammedan pilgrims, wading through immense deserts of suffocating sands, to pay their respects to the tombs of the Prophet. (*Co*, 17)

Webster was thus hardly an indifferent spectator. French experimentation in religious and moral life frightened him. He saw revolutionary measures that made divorce easier, that turned children against their parents, and that removed the traditional restraints on the passions as "demoralizing" (this was the only word ever coined by Webster). He concluded that without "the fear of a *supreme being* and *future punishments* . . . the people are let loose in the wide field of mental licentiousness. . . ." There was, however, still some optimism left in him. He believed that the French passions would cool and they would pull back from most of their radical experiments and embrace a rational religion—the belief in a supreme being was, after all, Webster thought, natural in men (*Co*, 19).

The state of the political system in France inspired different, but equally strong fears, in Webster. He believed that the Jacobin government stood only because of the external threat from the allied monarchies and the effective use of repression on its political enemies. When the external enemy disappeared, Webster predicted that the French government would retrace its steps to some earlier form; this process might produce a military government, and Webster came very close to forecasting the rise of Napoleon. His main concern, however, was the influence of faction in French politics. He advised France to install a powerful chief executive in the place of government by committees that were easy prey for the plots of various factions.

In what amounted to a series of concluding remarks, Webster summarized and explained his response to the French Revolution. He claimed that he was not "an enemy to liberty or republican government," but he had not "imbibed the modern philosophy, that rejects all ancient institutions, civil, social and religious as the impositions of fraud. . . ." The law and religion, particularly, were necessary institutions to control "a great part of mankind, necessitated to labor, and unaccustomed to read, or to the civilities of refined life, who will have rough passions. . . ." In a long note attached to the essay he defended "aristocracy" and "the well-born" as another restraint on the rough and passionate masses. Deference to those of "natural worth" was amply illustrated by the respect generated among Americans by a figure like Washington, and "this respect has hither to restrained the violence of parties." The worth of a Washington was "inborn," Webster thought, and he objected violently to the notion that all characteristics were learned. This implied a level of equality he was not willing to concede (*Co,* 34–36).

To some extent, Webster saw the situation in France in the context of his New England background. In opposition to the equality demanded by radicals in the French Revolution, he counterposed the deference accorded a few local dignitaries in New England. He felt that the "personal influence" of older respected citizens was "most remarkable in New England" and that "wherever it exists peace and concord distinguish the neighborhood." He acknowledged that such characters do not exist in every New England "neighborhood" and where they do not, "society is distracted with quarrels and parties, which produce an uncommon depravity of morals" (*Co,* 36).

Clearly Webster saw in the French Revolution fruitful lessons for the United States. Most important, Americans should learn that faction was the death of liberty. With one eye on the democratic-republican clubs that had recently arrived on the American scene, Webster scolded the private political associations that had played a central role in the French revolt. Because clubs were artificially strong, they had overwhelmed wiser individual voices at election time. To drive home the lesson he related the story of the factious dispute between the Romans Sylla and Marius over command of the army. His anxiety over the rise of factions was clearly rooted in the knowledge that pro-French and pro-British factions were evolving in the United States and that both were seeking to influence government policy. Roman history, Webster warned, showed that factions led to violence and disorder.

The "Conclusion" of the essay was a remarkable mixture of ideas and anxieties based on both the French and American situations. In many ways Webster overlaid his feelings about the American political experience in the 1780s on the French. During the American revolt the newly formed states had been united by the necessity of fighting an external enemy, and when the threat was removed, the states fell into a period of disunion and drift. Only the Constitution had saved the states from disaster. It was exactly this pattern that Webster applied to the situation in France. He believed that the external threat of the allied monarchies would be defeated and France would then have to face the internal reality of "a defective constitution and feeble laws." He warned the French that "enthusiasm, necessary to animate her citizens in time of war, will be a source of infinite disorder in time of peace. . . ." In order to head off this postwar chaos, the French must take two political steps: they must create a bicameral legislature to replace the volatile single chamber body, and they "must learn that the executive power must be vested in a *single hand* . . . the executive must have force and energy." What was good enough for the United States was, in Webster's mind, good enough for France. He projected onto France his fears and anxieties about the United States, and in both situations he saw order and stability rooted in the same political measures (*Co*, 40–41).

Of all Webster's political writings, the essay on the revolution in France is perhaps the hardest to interpret. More than anything else he wrote, it revealed a man in mid-passage. Webster showed undeniable signs of hopefulness about France; he understood that France, in order to escape the age-old grip of Catholicism and monarchy, must necessarily employ radical measures. His attachment to republicanism was still strong, but events in the United States and France had planted doubt and anxiety in his mind. Up to a point, he was able to keep the two countries separate, but in many respects they dissolved into one. Faction was faction, passion was passion, rabble was rabble, and order was order—in both France and the United States. While, to some extent, he was still an advocate of change, the essay revealed a man increasingly concerned about order and authority. This concern was not simply a response to the extraordinary events in France; it was a generalized response to the course of revolution in America as well.

By the mid-1790s men such as Webster were beginning to perceive that, along with a republican system, revolution produced changes in religion, social mores, and the political attitudes of the people. For Webster and many others, the change from monarchy to republicanism was reasonable and a cause for celebration; but they also believed that change, if successful, would require great virtue and self-control on the part of the people. When, in both America and France, some of the people appeared to reject the religious, social, and political foundations that were the basis of republicanism, Webster, and many other Federalists, became alarmed and began to defend the institutions under attack. In the essay on the French Revolution Webster began the shift from his position as an advocate of constitutional republicanism to a more defensive stance as an advocate of a humbling controlling religion, a social structure based on deference, and political devices that filtered and muted the voice of the people. This shift was foreshadowed in the Giles Hickory essays, but it only became clear when the religious and social innovations in France and their reflections in America pushed it to the fore.

Orations . . . 1798 and 1802

Between 1794 and 1802 nothing occurred to halt the slow but steady conservative drift of Webster's thought. As a newspaper man during these years, he was in daily contact with the rising level of political partisanship. Gradually he came to believe the people incapable of supporting a constitutional system of government. A number of events pushed him to this conclusion. The ferocious public condemnation of the Jay Treaty, the daily invective directed at the Federalist administration, and Webster's growing suspicion of French influence in the United States combined to convince him that the people were a rickety basis for a republic. Webster was most alarmed, however, by the rise of the Jeffersonian faction and their ultimately successful challenge to Federalist control of the government. Webster could find no justification for this sort of political conflict; he saw it not as a natural development in a representative system but rather as faction undermining order and authority. Jefferson became for Webster the symbol of all his fears; as a slave-holding Virginian, a deist, and the leader of a faction critical of the established government, Jefferson was perfectly suited to play the villain's role.

Webster's political position bewteen 1798 and 1802 was clearly expressed in two Fourth of July orations delivered to the citizens of New Haven. [12] In the first, Webster was still, in part, optimistic but it was a much transformed optimism when compared with his position in 1794. Europe, and especially France, were lost causes; a French victory in Europe would produce disaster because radical revolutionary ideas would then become established doctrine in all of Europe. If the monarchies were to win, such a victory would engender enormous and oppressive militarization under which Europe would groan for years. Webster concluded that "we may consider Europe as declining in improvement, and reverting back to the darkness and ferocity of the middle ages." Given this gloomy portrait, "the christian and lover of freedom" must look upon the United States as a haven to save and to foster the seeds of a pure church and excellent constitutions of government, which may hereafter be transplanted to Europe, when the hostile spirit of the present revolution shall have swept away all the old establishments" (1798, 10).

This role as haven required that Americans be especially vigilant. Webster suggested to his audience that they resist the ideas of the French Revolution and cling to the principles of "true religion and sound government" so that when peace returned to Europe the American example would be intact. The "cornerstone" of the American model (and of all truly republican governments) was "that the will of every citizen is controlled by the laws, or supreme will of the state," and if this principle falls "we are slaves." Webster advised the people that their duty to their country was to submit to and peaceably obey the laws, refraining from active political expression. Incredibly, he held up the American Revolution as an example of proper political action. Ignoring the important role mob action played in the American revolt, he portrayed it as "guided by wise and able men" and "scarcely was its progress disgraced by a popular tumult" (1798, 14).

If we compare the 1798 oration with that delivered in 1802 we discover a remarkable transformation. By 1802 Webster had become convinced that the American republic was doomed to failure. The United States, since the Revolution, had been beset by grave problems and disappointments. He claimed—neglecting Jefferson, Adams, and others—that the revolutionary generation was gone and that in their place was rising a generation of corrupt, self-serving, office seekers. A deep pessimism pervaded the 1802 speech. Webster had come to believe that the republican structures created in the 1780s and 1790s had little chance to survive. Reflecting the growing religious tones of his thought, he used biblical history to explain his position: "If Moses, with an uncommon portion of talents, seconded by divine aid, could not secure his institutions from neglect and corruption, what right have we to expect, that the labors of our lawgivers will be more successful?" (1802, 8)

He made it plain that constitutions, representation, and virtue, as Americans understood them, could not save the republic. Constitutions were little more than nothing in the contest with "the assaults of faction." With Jefferson in mind, he claimed that "against men who command the current of public confidence, the best constitution has not the strength of a cobweb." A representative system, he admitted, had some strengths; it reduced the chance that the people would assemble in a mob and convulse the state "but it neither humbles pride, subdues ambition, nor controls revenge and rivalry. It still left the state subject to the operation of all the turbulent, restless passions of man. . . ." Virtue, defined as "pure *morals*," would indeed be a safe foundation of a republic, but Webster sadly concluded that history offered no example of a morally pure nation (1802, 12).

To what did Webster attribute his gloomy forecast? For one thing, he saw the newspapers as a major cause of the people's discontent with government. To him, a newspaper editor himself, the "gazettes" were "a species of silent messengers walking by night and by day, stealing into farm houses and taverns whispering tales of fraud about public officers, exciting suspicion, spreading discontent, and weakening confidence in government." Next, Webster maintained that America was under the spell of a fallacious notion of equality. He admitted that equality of "life, limbs, reputation and property" was just, but there existed no justification for "an equal right to distinction and influence." Webster contended that a deferential elite was natural and necessary, but that the people were imbued with the absurd notion of absolute equality. Part of his attack on equality was an attack on the idea of equal suffrage. He claimed that since property was unequally divided the suffrage should reflect this fact. Because protecting property was "nineteen twentieths of all the objects of government," property owners should have some advantage when it came to voting. Webster implied that the people in general had to be as far removed from power as possible. Specifically, this meant longer terms for officeholders, no right to instruct representatives, and no extension of the suffrage since such a measure would "accelerate the growth of corruption." Finally, Webster believed that too many Americans thought "the officers of the government are the *servants of the people* and *accountable to them*." The tendency of this notion, he claimed, was "to degrade all authority, to bring the laws and officers of the government into contempt, and to encourage discontent, faction and insurrection" (1802, 8–16).

How can we account for this change in Webster's political thought? In the first place, it was not a total reorientation on his part. The faith in deference by the people to an elite and the desire to insulate the representatives from the direct control of the voters had appeared in the Giles Hickory essays more than a decade earlier. By 1802 the people had become considerably more threatening to him because of the violent partisanship of the 1790s and because they had elected Thomas Jefferson in 1800. Horrified by some of Jefferson's policies, Webster concluded that the transition of power from the Federalists to the Jeffersonians marked the beginning of the end. Specifically, he was critical of Jefferson's policy of replacing what Webster saw as good moral men with immoral types for solely partisan reasons. He was particularly incensed when Jefferson removed Elizur Goodrich from the post as Collector of the Port at New Haven, and installed Samuel Bishop in his place.

Webster wrote to both Jefferson and Madison, not long after the Jeffersonians had taken office, to complain about this specific appointment and the principle involved. In the letter to Jefferson, later published, Webster billed himself as "the 'still small voice' of truth" who wrote "without the remotest influence from personal irritations. . . ." The letter, however, was deeply imbued with a sense of personal outrage over the type of men Jefferson appointed. In part, his purpose was to protest the selection of Samuel Bishop, but the letter goes far beyond that local situation:

Your measures, Sir, invert the whole order of society. The natural sentiment of man is to respect virtue, religion, grave manners, eminent talents, the wisdom of experience, and the hoary head. Your practices tend to depress eminence of talents, to point the finger of scorn at a veneration of religion, to exalt the young over the head of the old, to discard solid worth, and to dignify with honors and emoluments of government the departed, the licentious and the profane. . . . If mankind can long endure this monstrous inversion of principles, of sentiments, and of habits—if they can lay aside their respect for age, wisdom, experience, and virtue, and look up with veneration to the illiterate, the debauchee, the blasphemer, the infidel—if they can calmly bear to see the hoary judge driven from the seat of justice to make way for the beardless tyro—the world has now the opportunity of determining these questions by the experiment, and on the event of this experiment depends the fate of your official character and of your administration.[13]

This letter helps explain the transition in Webster's position between 1798 and 1802. Before Jefferson's election Webster, while dismayed by the violent political battles in the United States and France, could take great comfort in the knowledge that men whom he saw as a natural aristocracy (Washington, Adams, and others) were at the helm. With the Federalist defeat in 1800 Webster's fears and anxieties had no counterbalance; the elite upon whom he staked so much was out of power, and the new administration was composed of men he could not trust. For Webster this crisis was much more than a political problem; it was profoundly moral as well. The new men in power were in Webster's view "men who openly revile and hold in contempt the religious institutions of their country—men who openly blaspheme the name and attributes of God and Jesus Christ—men who violate the laws and destroy the peace of their families by these and other atrocious crimes. . . ."[14] Thus Webster saw both the moral and political condition of the nation descending together; the despair present in his 1802 Fourth of July Oration was inextricably bound up with this perception.

Ten Letters to Dr. Joseph Priestly [sic]

When Webster retreated from New York to New Haven, he settled deep into New England's quiet bosom. New Haven, near the turn of the century, was a lovely city of elm-lined streets that led from the harbor to the Green where the State House, the church, and the cemetery stood as reminders of New England's interest in politics, religion, and death. To the west stood Yale College and memories of Webster's student days. Webster and his wife purchased the Benedict Arnold house from which they could watch the boats on

Long Island Sound and check the progress of the many fruit trees that surrounded the house. It was, all in all, a more familiar and comfortable environment than bustling, contentious New York. Irksome objects, however, still appeared on Webster's desk. Probably late in 1799 he read the *Letters to the Inhabitants of Northumberland* by Joseph Priestley and he was so enraged that a reply must have seemed like an obligation.

Priestley was an eminent character, an English Unitarian clergyman who made his mark by discovering oxygen in his second trade as chemist. He also wrote political tracts; his political views had compelled him to leave New England in 1794 and settle in Pennsylvania where he allied himself with the Jeffersonian party. Webster was unimpressed, and his reply to Priestley's 1799 analysis of American politics and culture was snide, rude, and insulting. In it Webster touched on a number of subjects and gave a fairly accurate portrait of his attitudes in the crucial year 1800.

The *Letters* were characterized, first of all, by a xenophobic tone often connected to Webster's traditional habit of portraying New England as the seat of true virtue and morality. He linked Priestley and William Cobbett, the English-born Philadelphia journalist, together as "foreigners and aliens" who should not "trouble the citizens of America with your pestiferous disputes or your arrogant pretensions to instruct them in their duty." Any more immigration of Europeans, Webster thought, would surely ruin the New World; the natural increase of population would suffice. Americans had no problem with peaceable and hard-working newcomers "but for every one such European we receive three or four discontented, factious men who, accustomed to quarrel with the unjust laws of their own countries, do not lay aside their opposition here, although the same evils are acknowledged not to exist."[15] In Webster's mind the New World was always seen in contrast with the Old. European nations were racked by political factions and conflicts; the New World should be a place of political and social harmony. On these grounds, men like Webster could argue for immigration restriction so that European revolutionary insanity could be kept in Europe.

In opposition to disruptive Europeans Webster placed the law-abiding, peaceful New Englander. Webster suggested that Priestley's views were incorrect because he lived near Philadelphia and mistook the attitude of the middle states for that of America. Priestley had seen only a small section of America, "and that part only in which the inhabitants have no national character. . . ." The middle states, Webster asserted, contain lower classes composed not of Americans, but Europeans. New England was America, it seemed, and Webster, at several points, suggested that only New Englanders were true Americans. Their political thought, for example, was based on a true understanding of constitutional government and what was meant by "a *representative republic.*" New Englanders "are independent landowners free and accustomed to manage their own local concerns, to choose their Representatives, to *respect them when chosen,* to *place confidence in them,* and *obey their laws.*" This, Webster informed Priestley, was not democracy. A democracy, according to Webster, was a government where the power was held directly by the people and not entrusted to representatives. Webster concluded:

Hence the word *Democrat* has been used as synonymous with the word *Jacobin* in France; and by an additional idea, which arose from the attempt to control our government by private popular associations, the word has come to signify a person who attempts an undue opposition to or influence over government by means of private clubs, secret intrigues or by public popular meetings which are extraneous to the constitution. By *Republicans* we understand the friends of our Representative Governments, who believe that no influence whatever should be exercised in a state which is not directly authorized by the Constitution.[16]

This statement illustrated several key aspects of Webster's thought. First, it clearly made the distinction between "democrat" and "republican"—a distinction central in Webster's mind. Second, notice Webster's desire to clearly define words; he believed that faulty definitions had caused great political troubles. Third, like many Federalists, he had insensibly blended France and the United States into one country. His definitions did grave damage to both the historical reality of Jacobinism in France and the "Democrats" in America. This sort of reductionism of complex events into simple formulas was a common practice among Federalists in the bitter years between 1798 and 1801.

The *Ten Letters* also gave Webster a chance to take a few shots at William Cobbett, who had been one of his main journalistic rivals. Priestley had asserted that Cobbett was one of the most popular writers in America. Webster assured Priestley that, in New England, Cobbett was hardly read at all. Peter Porcupine, as Cobbett was usually known, was devoted to "the British interest" and all his support came from that party. People in power, Webster contended, saw Porcupine for what he was, a scandalmonger whose pro-British position made it easier for the opposition to Federalist government to claim the existence of a plot to return the United States into the hands of monarchical Britain. If Cobbett had any influence it was "to excite uneasiness against Great Britain and against our government for its pacific policy toward Great Britain." Showing that he had learned a little invective himself in the 1790s, Webster claimed that people read Cobbett "for the same reason they would go to a mountebank" and that Cobbett's opinions "have no more weight than the howlings of a bulldog."[17]

In addition to political remarks, Priestley had also commented on American education and morals. Webster was forced to agree with the Englishman on several matters. In comparison to Europe, American higher education was a disgrace, virtually destitute of the necessary books and scientific apparatus. Using New England as an example, however, Webster claimed that learning was "more diffused among the laboring people than in any country on the globe." He also defended the United States as advanced in political learning and claimed that Europe could learn a great deal about correct politics from the New World.

Webster attempted to explain the generally poor state of learning and literature in America by attributing it to "the equal distribution of estates and the small property of our citizens. . . ." Both of these factors were crucial for republican government, but Webster also saw that they "actually tend to depress the sciences." Scholarship demanded money and leisure, and the middle-class society in America provided inadequate amounts of both. Furthermore, "our rage for gain absorbs all other considerations; science is a secondary object, and a man who has grown suddenly from the dunghill, by a fortunate throw of the die, avoids a man of learning as you would a tiger." This remark may well have been based on Webster's own experience. As a man who aspired to be "a man of learning" he may have felt a certain resentment toward those newly rich recently up from the "dunghill."

Yet while he had doubts about the present state of learning and science in America, Webster was still able to summon up the notion that America would one day equal the achievements of any nation. He insisted that Priestley acknowledge that great progress had been made in the New World. He painted a picture of a wilderness "converted into a garden and clothed with fruitful fields," of a country "covered with handsome towns and cities. . . ." All this was ruled by a government created and controlled by the people. To Webster, this was "the most precious tribute that mankind can receive from the new world, and ought of itself to rescue the character of its inhabitants from the imputation of dulness [*sic*] or barbarism."[18] So even at the height of his political despair Webster could still summon up a decent defense of America as an experiment in free government. He retained at least a remnant of the basic American belief that America was an experiment for the sake of all mankind.

Finally, Priestley had made the blunt charge that American morals were less pure than those in Europe. Webster agreed in part; he thought American lower classes had deplorable morals but that generally American morality was defensible. The problem with the lower classes stemmed from the nature of the American government and the higher wages paid in the United States. Despotism had its advantages; under it the lower classes had no political power and were "compelled to labor more hours and days for a subsistence than in our country." Thus, European working people have less time and money with which to pursue vice. In the end, Webster concluded, "industry does more to preserve morals than laws or sermons."[19]

The *Ten Letters* were the product of a retreating warrior, written from the haven of New England. They illustrate that Webster could write with a sneer. He wrote from the mountain top to those below; rarely in his life was he more didactic or arrogant. Priestley proved to be the calmer and more fair-minded man; he wrote Webster a reply in which he stated his love of the American Constitution and claimed that he had written only to defend himself against the stream of abuse coming from Cobbett. In the face of Webster's abuse Priestley remained calm and eventually gave high praise to Webster's work on epidemic and pestilential diseases.

Marcellus and Sidney

Between 1800 and his death in 1843, Webster devoted most of his energy to the study of language and the making of dictionaries. He only occasionally commented on political matters and then gave only fragmentary clarifications of past positions. Near the end of his life, in the late 1830s, he published four letters: one a short pamphlet signed "Marcellus," and the other three were signed "Sidney" and published in Webster's old papers the *Commercial Advertiser* and the *Spectator* now edited by William Leete Stone. Together they reflected Webster's growing despair over the drift of politics in the first four decades of the nineteenth century. They also show that since 1802 little had changed for Webster: he was appalled by the scramble for office and by the passions and unreliability of the people. If anything, he had grown more resolutely anti-democratic, seeking, as he had in 1802, devices to mute the voice and vote of the people.

As "Marcellus" and "Sidney," Webster made many of the same points he had made in 1802. The removal of men from appointed office as a new administration took over still incensed him; he claimed, for example, that "the doctrine that the *spoils belong to the victors* originated in savagism." He asked, "what is the difference in principle between the Gauls, who fought to rob their enemies of their cattle and their lands, and a political party that contends by all means, moral and immoral, for victory in election to strip their opposers and engross all the emoluments of government?"[20] He still objected to the notion that the representative was a mere agent of the people—an agent who must slavishly follow his constituents' instructions. He thought the people had become tyrants "just as bad as kings." In fact, they were often worse than kings since the people were "less restrained by a sense of propriety or by principles of honor . . ."; they were "more under the control of violent passions, exasperated by envy and hatred of the rich . . . and subject to no responsibility." He found it a "melancholy truth" that "the people will not create a power that shall restrain themselves from such excesses . . . they will not create a power which shall effectually defend their own personal rights and safety."[21]

If the people would not control themselves, Webster was willing to suggest changes that would lessen the role of popular tumult in politics. By 1837 the contest for president had become so contentious and involved with the spoils system that Webster proposed that "for the peace of society . . . that all executive and judicial officers should hold their offices during good behavior." This suggestion referred only to appointed officials, but Webster came very close to recommending that it apply to the president as well. He thought that the presidency was "a prize of too much magnitude not to excite perpetual dissensions; and if the contentions for the office . . . do not ultimately overthrow our Constitution it will be a miracle." He thought that a way could be devised to avoid this problem "but the practica-

bility of introducing such a mode is questionable." For similar remarks in one of his "Sidney" letters he was roasted by New Yorkers
as a monarchist—a charge he denied.[22]

If Webster had not become a monarchist, he had certainly become
a stout champion of the rich. He defended "rich capitalists" against
the charge that they were "drones in society, living on the industry
of the working bees." Webster saw the wealthy as supported by "the
fruits of their own industry. . . ." He also believed that wealthy men
were the only source "of great public improvements either by their
own investments or by loans to government. Such means cannot be
furnished by the poor." More important, Webster suggested that the
Congress be reorganized to recognize the different interests of prop-
erty-holders and non-property-holders. Since there existed no distinct
ranks or orders of men in America, it was difficult to balance the rich
and poor in the legislature. America could have no House of Lords,
so Webster suggested that the electorate be divided "into two classes,
the qualifications of one of which shall be superior age and possession
of a certain amount of property; while the other class of voters shall
comprehend those who have not the same qualifications." The two
groups of voters would be independent of each other, and their representatives would sit in different chambers, "each with a negative
upon the other." This suggestion was based on the idea from the
1802 oration that equal suffrage was essentially unequal since those
without property had the same vote as property owners. In 1837
Webster had come to see this as a question of rights. The wealthy
were concerned with the *"rights of property"* while the poor were most
interested in the *"rights of person."*[23] The representatives elected by the
older, wealthy citizens would defend property rights, the other chamber would protect personal rights.

Webster had come a long way since the 1780s. As a young man,
full of hope and a desire for change, he saw America as a stage where
mankind would create perfect or nearly perfect institutions. As time
passed, the play changed, and Webster grew less sure that America
could build the utopia he had envisioned in the 1780s. Two changes
in his thought were crucial: he gradually lost his faith in the good
character of the American people, and he came to fear the men who
began to enter American politics. By the late 1790s both of these
developments had reached a climax. The people too regularly clam-
ored against government actions such as neutrality and the Jay
Treaty, and they made it clear to Webster that political control was

going to be contested for on a regular basis. This constant conflict over political power ran counter to his deep faith in government by the wisest and best. While he never explicitly stated as much, Webster assumed that his utopian, republican America would have its basis in an educated, property-owning electorate who went dutifully to the polls and turned over power to an experienced, wealthy, and better educated elite who would govern unmolested until the next election. Events in the late 1780s and the 1790s taught him that the people would not give up power between elections; they formed clubs to influence government action, they read newspapers that ridiculed government, and they joined a party that contested the election of 1800 and won. Webster blamed the people for lack of virtue and steadiness and condemned the factious, discontented men like Jefferson who courted their votes. In the last analysis, Webster simply defined the American Revolution in terms that grew increasingly anachronistic. Americans generally saw persistent party conflict as a proper means of settling issues; Webster, on the other hand, saw things differently:

It is to be wished that the men in power in United States . . . would quit the business of abusing each other and their fellow citizens with party names and hard words. . . . I will tell you what we all want. We want a *wise government*, and we *want law*. It was for *these* the men of the Revolution fought and suffered; it was for *these* our fathers adopted a republican form of government; and if the government does not provide and secure to us *these blessings*, the Constitution is a failure.[24]

Chapter Four
The Prompter

Webster's life as an author has very little unity to it. No long-term purpose or enduring commitment stands out as his grand passion. He wrote schoolbooks, political pamphlets, essays on language, dictionaries, and even dabbled in science. Never during his life was he able to focus all his energies on any one of his many interests. He was perhaps, above all, a talented dilettante, never achieving real competence in anything he attempted. If we can trust the scholars who have tried to appraise his career, two areas of endeavor seem to dominate in his life—his schoolbooks and the dictionary. In most cases these two have been selected because they fit neatly with the simplistic notion that Webster was driven only by burning nationalism. Both the school texts and the dictionaries, some scholars claim, were sold to the public with flourishes of nationalistic rhetoric laced with Webster's obsession that Americans should learn from American books.

This chapter, however, is devoted to another aspect of Webster's life—one that has been often underemphasized. Between 1787 and 1798 Webster was for the most part a journalist, exploring the role of newspapers, magazines, and popular nonfiction in the new republic. He entered this period as a twenty-nine-year-old full of energy and optimistic about America and Americans. He emerged in 1798, nearly forty, his optimism broken and moving quickly toward the pessimism and bitterness that characterized his later years. During this period he produced a year's run of a notable magazine: *The Prompter,* a charming and much-overlooked little volume; he also edited one of the major newspapers in New York and produced a major scientific work on the nature of disease and epidemics.

The American Magazine

In the autumn of 1787 Webster gave up his teaching position in Philadelphia and moved to New York to seek the status and steady income that had eluded him for so long. The inspiration to found a magazine was not long in coming. In Philadelphia, Matthew Carey and Francis Hopkinson had established *The Columbian Magazine* and it had achieved something approximating success. In New Haven, Webster's Yale classmate, Josiah Meigs, was editing the *The New Haven Gazette* and *The Connecticut Magazine* that soon became an outlet for the satire of the Hartford Wits. New York City, Webster realized, was growing and would quickly come to dominate commerce and have a growing influence on American intellectual life—and it had no magazine.

After making a deal with Samuel Campbell, under which Webster sold the rights to his three schoolbooks for ready cash, he signed an agreement with Samuel Loudon to print a magazine. The venture lasted a year, finally dying from lack of subscribers and ready capital to support the magazine during its infancy. During its short life the *American Magazine* was too often a random assortment of short pieces hastily composed by Webster or borrowed from other American or British publications. For example, the first issue (December 1787) contained pieces called "Titus Blunt on Fashion" and "Anecdote of the Duke of Gordon," both probably written by Webster. It also featured a London review of John Adams's *Defence of the American Constitution*. Webster printed a considerable number of bad poems including "The Rare Adventures of Tom Brainless . . ." and "The Virgin's First Love." Some of this poetry was his own. The January 1788 issue began with the following effort by the editor entitled "Verses on the New Year":

> The circling Sun, bright Monarch of the day,
> Who rules the changes of this rolling sphere,
> With the mild influence of his favoring ray,
> From shades of night calls forth the opening Year.
>   Propitious Year! O may thy light divine
> Dispel the clouds that this new world impend,
> On infant States with peaceful lustre shine,
> And bid their fame o'er all the world extend.
>   Hail, blest COLUMBIA! whose embattled meads
> The crimson streams, of Heroes' blood have dy'd,
> Here see bright turrets rear their lofty heads,
> And domes of slate adorn thy rising pride.
>   Thy noble sons, with generous ardor fir'd,
> Shall gild the victories of their father's arms;
> They blooming Fair, in innocence attir'd,

Shall deck thy glories with unnumber'd charms.
Now ARTS shall flourish in this Western clime,
And smiling COMMERCE triumph on the main,
The fields shall blossom in perpetual prime,
And fruit's luxuriant robe the verdant plain.
These are the prospects of thy golden days—
These the glad hopes that cheer each joyful face.
Fly swift thou Sun; diffuse thy peaceful rays,
And give these blessings to our fond embrace.

Webster would have been well advised to leave all the poetry to others. Politics and education were his strong suits.

The magazine also sought to be utilitarian, presenting pieces on the ingrafting of fruit trees and the proper way to construct a chimney. Politically, the *American Magazine* was staunchly Federalist. Webster, writing under the name Giles Hickory, criticized the antifederalist faction for wanting a Bill of Rights attached to the Constitution (see chapter 2). The most interesting series in the magazine was Webster's essay on education that appeared in installments beginning with the first issue.

During his tenure as editor of the *American Magazine* Webster often tried his hand at literary criticism. His most notable review (July 1788) was of Timothy Dwight's *The Triumph of Infidelity;* a work that Webster clearly misunderstood. There was not much that he liked about the poem which he found a "jumble of unmeaning epithets . . ." and he criticized, particularly, the author, unknown to Webster, for his shabby treatment of the Chinese religion. The review was seriously flawed by Webster's inability to distinguish between the author's own views and those that Dwight put into the mouth of Satan or his henchmen. The review was so unfair that Dwight severed his relationship with Webster. Dwight was probably unfair in responding so violently; Webster's view of the poem was not vindictive, it was more the product of an overworked editor who did not have time to read carefully the long and difficult work and give it serious consideration.

As important as its contents was Webster's conception of what the magazine was to be. In the introduction to the first issue he explained to his readers what he was trying to do. The *American Magazine* was designed to be a national publication; it would concern itself with news from all sections of the country. Webster largely made good on this promise by presenting a section in each issue called "American

Intelligence," composed of edited pieces from a wide range of American newspapers (there was also a section for "European Intelligence"). America, in the editor's view, needed such a national magazine because "while we allow foreign publications all their merit, it must be conceded that none of them can be wholly calculated for this country." Webster also set himself the difficult task of producing a magazine that would "gratify every class of reader—the Divine, the Philosopher, the Historian, the Statesman, the Moralist, the Poet, the Merchant and the Laborer."[1] Special attention would also be given to female readers. In essence, Webster sought to create a national democratic magazine; one that would interest all sections of the country and all classes in society. He was, in the end, unable to achieve his noble goal. The result was a magazine that most often resembled a cut-and-paste effort by an inexperienced editor desperately short of copy.

When Webster realized that the magazine would not succeed, he made an attempt to secure more financial backing by taking in a number of partners from almost every state. He proposed that men such as Benjamin Rush, Jeremy Belknap, Joel Barlow, and James Madison become a set of proprietors who would invest in the magazine and collect original materials from their parts of the nation. When this plan failed, Webster gave up the magazine, left New York, and moved to Hartford.[2] The *American Magazine* stands as one of the few attempts made during the 1780s and 1790s to issue a publication based on nationalistic and republican principles. Webster's failure to lure a significant audience at least suggests that the time had not yet come for such a magazine.

The Prompter

During most of Webster's life his work appeared regularly in newspapers. Often he wrote what amounted to letters to the editor, but he also used the papers as an outlet for other work. A prime example were the essays that eventually became one of his most popular books—*The Prompter*. Between December 1790 and June 1791 Webster published sixteen essays in the *Connecticut Courant,* later adding nine new pieces to make up the book. All the essays were in the manner of Franklin's Poor Richard. They feature short sentences, plain style, and use familiar situations to illustrate moral lessons. The best selections employ humor and simple stories to satirize common failings and vices. Webster also offered advice on manners, morals, and domestic economy. The book first appeared in a Hartford edition printed by Hudson and Goodwin in late 1791. It enjoyed widespread success in the United States and Great Britain. Between 1791 and 1850 *The Prompter* was reprinted some fifty times in various versions, and parts of the little volume were often pirated and used as newspaper filler copy. Until 1796, for reasons unknown, Webster did not acknowledge it as his work and his name did not begin to appear on the title page until 1798.

The Prompter has been unfairly overlooked by scholars who too often emphasize the dictionaries and schoolbooks. This little book revealed a great deal about Webster. In the first place, Webster confessed his own sense of the role he would like to play in society: the prompter, "the man who, in plays, sits behind the scenes, and looks over the rehearser, and with moderate voice, corrects him when wrong, or assists his recollection. . . ." Webster saw this role as "very necessary" and as one in which he could do "much good." This was more than an author's pose; it was a reflection of Webster's belief that although he was not cut out for public office, he was suited to act as judge of the morals and the behavior of "the numerous actors upon the great theater of life. . . ."[3]

While there was a measure of presumption in this attitude, he carried it off in a subtle and inoffensive way. The prompter decided to put his advice to the people in a unique way. "He wanted to whip vice and folly out of the country—he thought of Hudibras and M'Fingal—and pondered well whether he should attempt the masterly style of those writings." But he found satire unsuitable and turned to the style "of sober moral writers, and the pompous flowing style of modern historians." This in turn Webster rejected because "one half of his readers would not understand him" and his purpose was to do "as much good as possible, by making men wiser and better." He finally settled on a style he called "good solid roast beef" because "it sits easily on the stomach" (*Pr,* 1794, 6–8). His final choice turned out to be a reasonably good imitation of Franklin's Poor Richard's plain style.

Using this style, Webster produced a series of essays full of utilitarian advice. The first piece, for example, tells the story of Jack Lounger and his problems with a fireplace. Jack, it seems, is too fond of his bellows; he piles coals and wood on the hearth and blasts away with a bellows. Jack manages to produce a small blaze that quickly dies and a room full of smoke. Billy Trim, on the other hand, "has attended more to the principles of nature" and carefully builds a fire so that natural air currents soon produce a bright, warm fire. The moral of the story is *"common sense is money."* The second essay ("Green Wood will last longer than Dry") was further advice on the crucial subject of fire-building (*Pr,* 1794, 9–11).

Often the prompter's advice touched on subjects about which Webster clearly had firsthand experience. He strongly condemned the practice of dividing a small farm among the farmer's sons because they would not be able to live a decent life "on these mutilated farms." This advice no doubt reflected his father's experience in Connecticut. Webster's lack of success as a lawyer was probably the reason he believed, "let lawyers multiply till a famine of business come upon them, and then they will die like Egyptian frogs" (*Pr,* 1794, 23, 20).

Advice and suggestions fly thick and fast; Webster considered no aspect of life as too small for comment. He often began with a simple aspect of daily life and worked his way to a larger lesson. Farmers who did not plan well were called "do-for-the-present-folks" and often, in his view, did "double their necessary labor." Failure to return tools to their proper place was, according to the prompter, not a small sin because it involved lost time when the tool was needed again:

This time is lost, for it breaks in on some other business—the loss of this small portion of time appears trifling; but slovens and sluts incur such losses every day; and the loss of these little scraps of time determine a man's fortune. Let the Prompter make a little calculation—A farmer whose family expends one hundred pounds a year, if he can clear ten pounds a year, is a thriving man. In order to get his one hundred and ten pounds, suppose he labors ten hours a day: In this case, if he loses an *hour* every day, in repairing the carelessness of the day before, (and every sloven and slut loses more time than this, every day, for want of care and order) he loses a tenth part of his time—a *tenth* part of his income—this is a *eleven* pounds. Such a man cannot thrive. . . . (*Pr,* 1794, 27–28)

Such little sermons were more important than they first appear. The prompter was teaching time-thrift, a modern characteristic, largely unknown among rural people who adjusted their lives to the regular rhythms of nature. Webster was suggesting that the clock was more important to the American farmer who should put success and growth beyond mere self-sufficiency. The prompter was clearly a capitalist urging his readers to work hard, save, and expand: "If you have but a small piece of land, cultivate it well, make it produce as much as possible; and if you can get more than will maintain you from this little farm, lay out the surplus in buying more. If you cannot get more than a subsistence, it is time to think of lessening expenses, or selling out and buying new land" (*Pr*, 1794, 34).

Such expansive capitalistic attitudes were to have an important place in American history. The conservative habits of rural life left little room for speculation or growth. Franklin's Poor Richard and Webster's Prompter—advocates of saving, time-thrift, and gradual expansion—promoted America's change from a static agrarian society to a dynamic industrial nation. It would be wrong, however, to see Webster as having both feet in the modern age. His beliefs about thrift and saving owe as much to his Puritan ancestors as they do to his conception of the needs of a modern nation. Books such as *The Prompter* show Webster translating the seventeenth-century Protestant ethic into a usable formula for the nineteenth century.

Webster sought to instruct his fellow Americans on more than domestic economy. Several pieces, for example, discussed education of children. In these Webster revealed modern attitudes largely devoid of the Puritan emphasis on the innate evil of the young. Most of his comments assumed that if parents provided a just and loving environment for their children, all would turn out well. He sincerely believed that children would respond consistently to rational parents who dealt consistently with them. Good parents used punishment to correct faults, not simply to break their children's wills. *The Prompter* did not assume that children had an innate tendency to evil; instead, he maintained "that *nine* times out of *ten*, the bad conduct of children is owing to parents! Yet parents father most of it upon Adam and the devil" (*Pr*, 1794, 37).

As the prompter, Webster was, as usual, didactic and moralistic, but he pulled it off with a light and humorous touch that contrasted sharply with the heavy humorless approach he often adopted in his other writings. He was even capable of seeing that his views were necessarily subjective: he had the prompter claim, "And no way is so good as *mine*. The question is not, whether this or that is the *better* way, but whether it is *my* way or *your* way. Orthodoxy is *my* doxy, and heterodoxy is your doxy" (*Pr*, 1794, 68). The whole production was light and readable, the prompter's readers were preached at, but generally they never knew it.

Yet as we have seen, Webster changed a great deal during the 1790s. The popular protests against American neutrality and the Jay Treaty among other events had a profound impact on him. The excesses of the French Revolution seemed particularly significant to Webster, and the decade was topped by Jefferson's election. All of these influences turned Webster into a much more negative and frightened man. His political position became more conservative and his faith in the people's ability to participate in political affairs gradually declined.

The Prompter offers an excellent illustration of his metamorphosis. In 1803 Webster produced a revised edition of the little book that had been so popular for more than a decade. In addition to some minor changes in the original text, he added nineteen new essays, all of them radically different in style and content from his 1791 version. The titles of the new pieces reflected the change in Webster. The original essays often had coy and ambiguous titles; the new ones are straightforward and somber. They include "The Counsels of Old Men Despised, or, Revolt and Division of Empire," "Popular Discontent," and "Inconstancy of the Populace."

The new essays also showed a remarkable change in style. Webster cast aside Poor Richard's plain style in favor of a tone that most closely resembled sermonizing. Several times he used a story to illustrate his point, but instead of familiar tales of everyday life he employed biblical illustrations such as the history of the Jews and the story of Cain and Abel. The light satirical tone gave way to a straightforward didactic style. In "The Counsels of Old Men Despised, or, the Revolt and Division of Empire," Webster bluntly stated his feeling that "the ruler shun the advice of proud and headstrong youth—and let the people shun their flatterers, as devils in human shape" (*Pr,* 1803, 121). The reader was bludgeoned with the moral as Webster added lectures and sermons to a book of fables and tales.

More important, the change in the 1803 edition of *The Prompter* provides a chance to gauge the transformation in Webster's thought. It is very important to realize that alterations in his ideas were almost always a matter of degree rather than kind. In 1791, for example, Webster believed that children could be properly trained if parents

used mild and rational restraint. By 1803 he still was deeply interested in restraints, but he had profoundly altered his view about the
nature and severity of the restraint needed. In the essay, "Parental
Indulgence," he employed the biblical story of David and Adonijah
to show that mild treatment of a child will lead to disaster—Adonijah attempted to usurp David's throne. Webster thought the lesson
was clear: "This story is a fine satire on the modern system of education, which rejects the most salutary restraints, for checking the
growth and expansion of the intellectual faculties, and making children bashful and clownish. This mode however has been adopted by
honest people, who have not suspected that this is one of the means
devised to undermine the foundations of civil order" (Pr, 1803, 114).

Most of the 1803 essays that touched on education were based on
a new assumption. Webster had come to believe (given his experience
in the decade just past) that children, indeed human beings in general, were more passionate and obstinate than he had thought in
1791. Put another way, he had come to appreciate more fully the
innate evil in man. Essentially an optimist in the early 1790s, he had
by 1803 grown sour about man's prospects. This change, for instance, took the form of an increased sense that human history was
cyclical and that "the glory of nations is destined to fade before the
incessant attacks of time and corruption." To Webster the course to
steer was obvious; nations must turn away from sinful youth and let
the affairs of state "be administered by elderly men, who have acquired wisdom by experience" (Pr, 1803, 121).

Offering older, more experienced men as a bulwark against the
slide to corruption and decay was only a half-hearted hope. Just as
often Webster was capable of total despair: "No religion has been sufficient to control—no government or laws sufficient to restrain all the
evil propensities of men. What then will men be, when freed from
these restraints? Who is the projector of hardiness enough to risk the
experiment and commit the destinies of a nation to the 'self-govern-
ment' of individuals?" (Pr, 1803, 115–116). Webster believed that
America was in the process of launching just such as "experiment,"
and he was frightened. Still playing the part of prompter, he sought
to warn his readers of the imminent dangers. In 1791 he had been a
gentle prodder directing Americans toward lives of virtue; by 1803
the drama before him had changed, and the promptings sounded a
great deal like a prophecy of doom.

The *Minerva*

In 1793 Webster returned to New York to launch, for the second time, a journalistic venture. As an ardent Federalist, Webster was chosen by members of the party to edit a newspaper in New York that would counter the rising tide of antifederalist criticism spread by partisan sheets like the *New York Journal*. To get the project off the ground, a group of Federalist leaders, including John Jay and Alexander Hamilton, each lent Webster (interest free) one hundred and fifty dollars. By late summer 1793 Webster had created a printing company, and by November he was in New York ready to publish. The first issue appeared 9 December 1793.

The original name was *The American Minerva, patroness of peace, commerce and the liberal arts*. In March 1794 the name was changed to *American Minerva, and the New York (Evening) Advertiser*. In May Webster announced the creation of *The Herald*, a country weekly that deleted most of the city-oriented advertising and condensed and reorganized the copy from the daily city editions. These were significant innovations and Webster was apparently among the first to employ them. It allowed him to sell twice copy that had been expensively typeset, and it expanded his circulation, carrying the news to people who usually had no newspaper. In 1797, after several more name changes, the two editions took the titles *Commercial Advertiser* and *Spectator*.

The venture was one of Webster's successes. After a slow start, circulation began to grow—as did advertising revenues—and he was able to pay off the loans that had allowed him to start the paper. The reasons for his rise are not hard to understand. Even in the 1790s most papers were still edited by glorified printers. Webster, with his college education, experience in journalism, and a reputation gained through his textbooks, was in an ideal position to publish a paper superior to most of his competition. This was part of an important change in American journalism. Papers were being edited rather than simply printed. Editors were becoming public figures. At about the same time Webster created the *Minerva,* other men with considerable talents were moving into journalism. Benjamin Franklin Bache, William Cobbett, and Philip Freneau, like Webster, were men of literary and intellectual skill who turned to journalism. They were editors who stamped their views and personalities on the papers they controlled. In the process they helped change American journalism from a world of news sheets to a world of newspapers.

Webster made his position as editor clear. He insisted upon his independence for, as he put it, "the complexion . . . of the paper has been given by myself, and I alone am responsible for the tenor of the *opinions* it contains." He stated the facts as he found them "without regard to party." "The National Government" had been "incorrupt and according to the spirit of the Constitution"—the *Minerva* defended its actions. While European powers battled, he defended American neutrality "because there has appeared no occasion for war, but great advantages in peace." Caught up in national and international disputes, he remained a true son of New England. Webster claimed that his principles were "those which prevail generally in the state which gave me birth and among the northern people."[4]

The finest, and perhaps the best-known, example of his journalism was the so-called Curtius letters. This series of long editorials began in October 1794 when the *New York Journal* published a violent attack on John Jay and his conduct of the negotiations with England that sought to settle trade relations and the problem of Great Britain's continued presence in the American northwest. On 28 October a letter appeared in the *Minerva* defending Jay, and after nearly a year of increasingly bitter exchanges, the *Minerva* printed a series of twelve articles signed "Curtius" that sought to vindicate the Jay Treaty. They reappeared in the *Herald* and were widely reprinted in other Federalist papers.

These pieces would be out of place on today's editorial page. They were technical, densely reasoned, and overly long. Webster devoted a good deal of space to answering technical objections to the treaty. On the positive side he argued that America was in no position to compel England in any way. The treaty, in Webster's view, was the best deal available, given the realities Jay faced. In the end Webster called on the people to trust and pay deference to leaders like Jay and Washington: "Is there a shadow of reason to believe that men grown grey in the service of their country, whose patriotism and virtue were never suspected, have now in the evening of life . . . commenced to be traitors. . . . You have not been deceived."[5]

The Curtius letters were important because they so often evoked the concept of deference. Webster, as a product of Connecticut, took it as an article of faith that leaders merited trust and deference from the people. Yet, ironically, Webster and the *Minerva* were involved in the process that was quickly undermining that deferential world. In the 1790s the idea of opposition to government rested on no very firm foundations, but they were being built. Newspapers began to criticize the actions of government and to do so in an increasingly partisan and violent way. Webster had, of course, been enlisted to counter just such criticism, and he never really accepted the legitimacy of opposition. In fact, he was so anxious about the inflammability of the public mind that he came to believe "that there must be something wrong in *principle* in opposition."[6] To the end of his career as journalist he never understood that, as a partisan for the people in power, he helped to spawn partisan journalism in America. Since Webster's day most defenders of the government have come to see the partisanship in their actions. Webster never did. As a zealot, he saw himself defending truth and order against opposition and anarchy.

Webster left journalism for two reasons. Eventually, he was forced to sell his interest in the papers because he had incurred the wrath of Alexander Hamilton. Webster had supported Adams against Hamilton during the 1800 breakup of the Federalist Party, and Hamilton sought his revenge by financing a second Federalist paper (the *New York Evening Post*) in New York. Under this competitive pressure Webster sold his holdings and in 1803 washed his hands of the newspaper business. Long before that time his enthusiasm for the business had waned. In 1798 he had withdrawn from active participation in the paper's production, writing only the political columns. He was worn out; his wife recalled that "his labors were incessant . . ." and when he finally left journalism to return to New Haven, "he was in a critical condition, mentally and physically." He had marched off to New York in search of the rostrum from which he could lecture the American public; he withdrew convinced the people were well on their way to ruin.[7]

A Brief History of Epidemic and Pestilential Diseases . . .

During Webster's career as journalist he became involved in the raging controversy over the cause and treatment of epidemics. Most of America's major cities had suffered outbreaks of yellow fever during the 1790s. Noah, with a lifelong layman's interest in science, threw himself into the study of epidemics with the same energy that he exhibited in all his other endeavors.

American physicians offered two theories to explain the epidemics. One school, led by Dr. Benjamin Rush, believed that yellow fever was of local origin, arising out of unsanitary conditions; the other school, led by Dr. William Currie, believed the disease was imported. Webster set out to make his contribution to the debate.

He first tirelessly collected historical information on epidemic diseases. He wrote to his long list of contacts in the United States and abroad asking for any personal testimony they might give regarding yellow fever or other pestilential diseases. He questioned sailors and others who arrived in New York; he sent out circular letters to prominent figures; and, in time, he had amassed a huge file of data on epidemics. These data were first published in 1799 as a series of twenty-five letters that appeared in the press. The major product, however, was a two-volume work, *A Brief History of Epidemic and Pestilential Diseases* . . . printed by Hudson and Goodwin in New Haven in 1799.

The crux of this massive work was the notion that yellow fever was caused by the condition of the atmosphere. Webster believed that natural phenomena such as abnormally mild winters or hot damp summers were the primary causes of epidemics. The first volume of the work was given over to a correlation of such natural events as earthquakes, meteors, eclipses, and meteorological quirks with the outbreaks of epidemic diseases. Beginning with Moses, Webster carried his history up to 1799. In the second volume he essentially made the argument that his researches proved a connection between the quality of the air and the outbreak of disease.

Webster, of course, knew nothing of microorganisms and their role in epidemics. So, in a sense, he was combing a haystack that contained no needle. Without this knowledge Webster, nor any of his fellow workers in the area, could have identified the mosquito as the carrier of the contagion. In retrospect his labors seem almost pathetic. Yet they were part of the slow painful process of scientific discovery. Beyond that, his work in science illustrated several important qualities about Webster during the 1790s. He was trying almost desperately to be of service to his nation. Yellow fever was probably the most fundamental health problem faced by the new nation and he wanted to help solve it. Also he was a child of the Enlightenment. The pages of his work on diseases were illuminated by a faith in progress based on historical study and research. The Enlightenment mind may be nearly impossible to define, but it surely contained a firm belief that tomorrow could be materially better than yesterday. In his labors on epidemics Webster was living out that belief.

Webster spent most of the 1790s as a journalist. This portion of his life has been obscured by those years spent working, first on his schoolbooks, and then later, on the famous dictionary. As a newspaperman, he helped American journalism come of age, and he played a crucial part in the process that brought the editor out of the printshop and into a new role in politics. He produced, in *The Prompter*, perhaps his most readable and lovable book. His researches on yellow fever, that grew naturally out of his journalistic activities, were one of the major contributions by an American to epidemiology. By the end of the decade, however, there were clear signs that he was changing. His faith in the people was crumbling, his belief in progress was somewhat shaken—he had begun to grow bitter and disillusioned.

Chapter Five
Language

Language should probably be listed with politics and religion as a subject to avoid in polite conversation. Debates over the proper pronunciation and usage of words seem to provoke violent emotions. Webster's career was a graphic illustration of this principle; from the mid-1780s until his death he was never far removed from often arcane battles over proper spelling, pronunciation, grammar, and the nature of language. He wrote spellers, grammars, essays on the nature of language, and, of course, dictionaries. In the process he revealed himself and some of the motives that drove him to work long hours on the dry and often sterile subject of words. A close reading of his work in language reveals a man with strong nationalist sentiments, but also a man with great respect and love for Britain. Webster sought to correct error and stamp out corruption in language, but he also believed that a language grew organically and that no man should or could stand in its way. He often expressed his dislike of regional dialects while attempting to establish New England speech and spelling as the national standard. If he was often confused and sometimes simply wrong, Webster nevertheless made a significant contribution to the study of language in America. Yet it was not the contribution of a narrow-minded scholar, but rather that of a man caught up in the passions of the time and his own personality.

Dissertations on the English Language

As a young man in the 1780s, Webster was excited about the American Revolution and the possibility that changes in politics would lead to changes in cultural affairs. He also desperately wanted to make a place for himself in the new republic as a man of authority and influence. He wrote on politics and education, seeking a voice for himself in the public debate over what America should do with her newly won freedom. He also quite naturally began to think about language and its role in revolutionary America. His schoolbooks called for an American language as free from European control as possible. Soon he began lecturing on language to groups in various American cities, propounding one fundamental principle: reject English authorities, speak and write American English. Although he began his career as a language reformer seeking to "clean up," "standardize," and "regularize" English, beneath his calls for reform there was also clear evidence of a conservatism, a need for order, that would grow stronger as the years passed.

This curious blend of conservatism and reform was evident in *Dissertations on the English Language* which appeared in 1789. In this work Webster reproduced five of his lectures along with numerous notes and an appendix calling for a reformed system of spelling. He included dissertations on the general history of language, on the elements of language, on corruptions and controversies, on the formation of language, and finally one on the construction of English verse. Their titles, however, hide the fact that the reprinted lectures were full of Webster's growing body of prejudices about language.

To understand these prejudices one must understand the influence of Horne Tooke on Webster. Apparently Webster read Franklin's copy of Tooke's *Diversions of Purley* late in 1786, and he never fully escaped from its influence. The book gave Webster a weapon with which to battle those who would structure English according to the rules of Latin. It also gave him a weapon to fight off such English authorities as Samuel Johnson and Bishop Robert Lowth who dominated language theory in America. From Tooke, Webster learned that English was rooted in the Saxon language and had developed slowly on its own until French influences after the Norman invasion and pedants like Johnson began to twist the language to conform to Latin grammar. Tooke was wrong and Webster inherited a number of misconceptions from him but the Englishman also gave Webster a fresh and exciting view of language. Webster came to see language as the product of growth rooted in the human mind and the environment. Webster, under Tooke's influence, took an historical approach to language that, while it produced some mistakes, shattered the notion that absolute rules could hold a language in place for any length of time.

Webster rode these insights for all they were worth. As an American seeking cultural independence, he used Tooke's theory to condemn most great authorities and set himself up as the possessor of truth. The language rules taught to American children were worse than useless because "had the English never been acquainted with

Greek and Latin they would never have thought of one half the distinctions and rules which make up our English grammars." Thus, in
his own words the main purpose of the *Dissertations* was "to restrain
the influence of men, learned in Greek and Latin, but ignorant of
their own tongue; who have laboured to reject much good English,
because they have not understood the original construction of the
language."[1]

While Webster revolted against the tyranny of Latin rules, he did
not advocate unhindered growth for the language. The standards that
he suggested were "the *rules of the language itself* and the *general practice
of the nation. . . .*" At another point he contended that language
should be controlled, in most cases at least, by the "principle of analogy." By this he meant that similar combinations of letters should be
pronounced the same whenever they appear. He also argued that
standards of proper speech should not be based "on the practice of
any particular class of people. . . ." Such elitism was "like fixing a
lighthouse on a floating island" (22–23, 25–27).

Indeed, it is very difficult to grasp exactly what Webster wanted
for American English. Did he want rules established by analogy, by
general practice, or by some inherent dynamic in the history of the
language? One thing is clear: he wanted Americans to speak as uni-
formly as possible. This desire had clear political roots; he not only
wanted the federal Constitution to bind the people together but he
also believed that "our political harmony is therefore concerned in a
uniformity of language." America in 1789 was in an ideal position to
establish such uniformity; Americans had been aroused by the Revolution to question European authority but even more they were prone
"to embrace any scheme that shall tend . . . to reconcile the people
of America to each other, and to weaken the prejudices which oppose
a cordial union." To create this uniformity would not be difficult because America had something that Europe did not—isolation. America was a linguistic island safe from the corruption of other languages
and already amazingly uniform in speech, especially compared with
England where "the people of distinct counties . . . can hardly understand one another, so various are their dialects." Webster guessed
that in America no more than a hundred words (mostly derived from
occupations unknown in other sections) were not "universally intelligible" (36, 289).

Why was this true? Webster got an answer to this question from
Horne Tooke and from his own conception of American life. Webster

believed English as spoken in England was corrupted and that "Chaucer, Shakespeare and Congreve . . . wrote in the true English stile [*sic*]." The language of New England, "except in a few commercial towns," was in Webster's opinion surprisingly similar to the older, purer English. For one hundred and sixty years New England "has been in the situation of an island," untainted by "any of the causes which effect great changes in language and manners." Webster was a revolutionary, but a revolutionary of an unusual sort. He found his golden age not in the future but in the past. The isolated villages of New England had retained not only superior social and political forms, but they also spoke and wrote a superior brand of English. The sense that England was failing, that corruption was rife, had been an important element in American thought since the early seventeenth century. Webster extended the notion to include language in that indictment of the rejected mother country (108).

The language of New England was not, however, perfect. New England yeomen had the unfortunate habit of pronouncing an *e* before an *r* like an *a* (*marcy* for *mercy*). But generally Webster defended the speech of New England against its critics. In addition to isolation, Webster saw New England's speech habits as conditioned by "the nature of their government and distribution of property."

In New England, where there are few slaves and servants, and less family distinctions than in any other part of America, the people are accustomed to address each other with that diffidence, or attention to the opinion of others, which marks a state of equality. Instead of commanding, they advise; instead of saying, with an air of decision, *you must;* they ask with an air of doubtfulness, *is it not best.* . . . Not possessing that pride and consciousness of superiority which attend birth and fortune, their intercourse with each other is all conducted on the idea of equality, which gives a singular tone to their language and complexion to their manners. (107)

Beyond suggesting backcountry New England speech and language habits as a national standard, Webster also suggested that Americans could improve their language by reforming the way it was spelled. Again the need for this reform was based on a sense of corruption and decay in the language. To Webster, it was obvious that there should be as little difference between spelling and pronunciation as possible. Unfortunately, natural change produced by the "progress of science and civilization," the mixtures of language "occasioned by revolutions in England," and the "predilection of the learned for words of foreign growth and ancient origin" had generated far too many differences between spelling and pronunciation. Uniformity would have a number of advantages. Children would find the language easier to learn, but, more important, uniformity would enforce a single standard on every American, and it would "remove prejudice and conciliate mutual affection and respect" between the various sections of the country. A more rational form of spelling would reduce the size of books and other publications by employing fewer letters. "A capital advantage" of a reformed system was the encouragement it would give to the production of American books. As American and English orthography gradually grew apart, "English" books would soon have to be recast into "American" (396–97).

Webster denied the notion that reformers could make orthography perfectly regular and simple, but he believed that "great improvements may be made. . . ." His position asked for three basic changes. The first called for the elimination of silent or useless letters (*bread* becomes *bred*). The second created new, clearer combinations of letters to replace those combinations that were vague or indeterminate (*mean* and *chorus* become *meen* and *korus*). A third change would have Americans use a point or mark to indicate the exact sound of a letter or syllable to unite two letters into a new single character (such as in *o* and *w* in *cow*).

The idea that English orthography needed reform was not new when Webster made his proposals in the *Dissertations*. As early as 1768 Benjamin Franklin had put forth *A Scheme for a New Alphabet and Reformed Mode of Spelling*. While Franklin clearly understood the difficulties associated with any such reform in a basic tool such as language, he thought that "sometime or other it must be done."[2] In 1786 Webster submitted his ideas to Franklin who eagerly gave his approval to the new plan. By the time the *Dissertations* appeared, Webster had refined his plan to include the three basic changes just described. He attempted to put his plan into practice by printing his *Collection of Essays and Fugtiv Writings* (1790) using his reformed orthography. This volume was truly one of the oddities in the history of American printing. Take for example this paragraph from the preface:

The reader will observ that the orthography of the volume iz not uniform. The reeson iz, that many of the essays hav been published before, in the common orthography, and it would hav been a laborious task to copy the whole, for the sake of changing the spelling.

If Webster believed that "every possible reeson . . . for altering the spelling of wurds stil exists in full force,"[3] others thought differently. Ezra Stiles, president of Yale, believed that Webster had "put in the pruning Knife too freely for general Acceptance." Jeremy Belknap was less gentle, dubbing Webster "critick and coxcomb general of the United States." These criticisms hit their mark; after 1790 radical spellings disappear even from Webster's diary. George Krapp, historian of American English, has concluded that Webster was not made "of the stern stuff of which great reformers are made" and that Webster realized his spelling reforms "might cause him to be regarded as visionary and doctrinaire, a kind of reputation that would have been fatal to his influence and to the reputation of his elementary educational books."[4]

Thus the proposal for spelling reform and the other notions about language found in the *Dissertations* came to little in the long run. By the late 1780s Webster's radicalism had waned, and he had begun to moderate his positions on political and cultural issues. When his notions met severe criticism from members of the American establishment that he so much wanted to join, a natural moderating process took hold.

Be that as it may, why was he so interested in language in the first place? Primarily, his interest in words was an outgrowth of his schoolbooks which took root during his early days as a teacher. Webster had, however, another motivation: words were power and to control words was to have power. A little-noted piece by Webster called "A Dissertation concerning the Influence of Language on Opinions . . ." that appeared in the *American Magazine* gives an insight into his concern with language. In this essay he maintained that "truth and accuracy of thinking" were based on "a clear understanding of words." Too often, he thought, the meaning of words was left to "school boys," an unfortunate circumstance because "it can be proved that the mere *use of words* has led nations into error. . . ." The bulk of the essay was devoted to his clarification of the true meaning of such words as "God," "the Devil," "soul," "mind," "spirit," "trial by peers," and "inflation." In most of these cases Webster maintained that the public generally used the term incorrectly; he, however, had traced the word back to its true meaning. This desire to set himself up as the authority on the use of language and thus give himself a position of power in all areas of human action was a central reason for his devotion to the study of language.[5] The *Dissertations* and later the dictionaries were often confusing and contradictory. Webster moderated and changed his mind often, but after 1790 he never entirely abandoned the task of making the language his so that he might have leverage to direct American opinion.

A Compendious Dictionary of the English Language

Noah Webster began the nineteenth century by announcing his plans to make dictionaries. On 4 June 1800 the New Haven newspapers carried an item explaining his intention to complete his "system for the instruction of youth" by compiling a small dictionary for use in schools. There would also be two other dictionaries, "one for the counting house and a large one for men of science." Life in the New World had spawned a number of new words rooted in different legal systems and "modes of life." Because Americans own land and think about religion in ways far removed from the English style, Americans should "dismiss from the language . . . several hundred words. . . ."[6]

This announcement met with general condemnation. By 1800 Webster had become a controversial figure; his political, medical, and linguistic opinions were often the object of ridicule. His plan to produce a dictionary of the American language provoked a new flood of criticism. The *Aurora,* a Democratic Party newspaper, put the dictionary in the context of what it saw as Webster's disastrous career. Calling him an "oddity of literature," the *Aurora* found his spelling injurious to the schools, his spelling reforms "capricious" and "incompetent," his work on yellow fever worthless, and his political writing pompous. As for the dictionaries, the paper concluded that Webster's real motive was "to *make money* by a scheme which ought to be and will be discountenanced by every man who admires the classic English writers. . . ." Joseph Dennie, editor of the *Gazette of the United States* in Philadelphia, called Webster "a maniac gardener, who, instead of endeavoring to clear his garden of weeds . . . entwines them with his flowers." Dennie also wrote a series of letters designed to mock Webster's dictionary:

To Mr. noab Wabstur

Sur,

by rading all ovur the nusspaper I find you are after meaking a nue Merrykin Dikshunary; your rite, Sir; for after lookin all over the anglish Books, you wont find a bit Shillaly big enuf to beat a dog wid. So I hope you'll take a hint, a put enuff of rem in yours, for Oct 'tis a nate little kit of furniture for any Man's house so it 'tis.

Pat O'Dogerty

Massa Webser plese put sum HOMMANY and sum GOOD POSSUM fat and sum two tree good BANJOE in your new what-you-call-um Book for your fello Cytzen.

Cuffee

Warren Dutton, editor of the Federalist *Palladium* in Boston, asserted that Webster was hard working and well intentioned "but modesty . . . is not the leading feature of his literary character. . . ." The dictionary, according to Dutton, must either include only pure English words, in which case it was unneeded "as we already possess the admirable lexicon of Johnson, or else it must contain vulgar provincial words, unauthorized by good writers and, in this case, must surely be the just object of ridicule and censure." Finally, Dutton suggested that if Webster persisted in producing a dictionary, the *Palladium* would provide a title—"let, then, the projected volume of *foul* and *unclean* things bear his own christian name and be called NOAH'S ARK."[7]

Despite the ridicule, charges, and countercharges, Webster set to work writing his dictionaries. He had inherited the work of a number of men who had been laboring to produce better dictionaries for nearly a century. The notion of a dictionary had slowly evolved over the centuries prior to 1800. Perhaps the first dictionaries were made by scholars working on ancient Latin manuscripts. They would place definitions alongside difficult words, and soon these were collected into a *glossarium* or glossary. The word *dictionary* was first used by Sir Thomas Elyot in 1538 when he published his *Dictionaries Liber*. Dictionaries of the English language did not begin to appear until 1600 when Robert Cawdrey produced *The Table Alphabeticall of Hard Words*. In 1623 Henry Lockham extended the idea to include ordinary words. By the second decade of the eighteenth century the desire to produce a standard dictionary of the English language was strong. A landmark in this movement occurred in 1747 when Samuel Johnson contracted with a group of booksellers to write a dictionary. The booksellers advanced Johnson fifteen hundred pounds and gave him three years to complete the work. He took eight years and required a great deal more money before producing two enormous folio volumes seventeen inches long and three and one half inches thick. Between 1773 and 1791 William Kenrick, William Perry, Thomas Sheridan, and John Walker created dictionaries to compete with Johnson's. Johnson became the arbiter of proper definition and Walker of proper pronunciation; these two men and their books were Webster's windmills—the foreign authorities he sought to overthrow.

With ridicule all around him, Webster set to work creating an American dictionary to challenge the English domination of the language. The first fruit was *A Compendious Dictionary of the English Language* (1806). This smallish dictionary was actually the fourth dictionary written and printed by an American. In 1798 Samuel Johnson, Jr., the first president of King's College (now Columbia University), produced the first American dictionary. Two years later Johnson and John Elliott published *A Selected Pronouncing and Accented Dictionary*. Also in 1800 Caleb Alexander introduced his *Columbian Dictionary of the English Language*. Unlike Johnson and Elliott, Alexander boasted of his Americanism, but included only a very few American words. Like Webster, Alexander extolled the virtues of a standard American pronunciation.[8]

Although Webster's *Compendious Dictionary* was not an original work, it did strike several new themes that he would work out more fully in his later dictionaries. Webster, in the preface, revealed that he had first conceived of the idea to make a dictionary around 1783 when "Dr. Goodrich of Durham" had suggested that such a volume should be a part of his general plan for the education of American youth. The preface indicated that while Webster's dislike of foreign authorities was still strong, he had become much more conservative in his opinions about language.

His attack on earlier dictionaries and grammars was still based on Tooke's notion that English was derived from Saxon. Because he had studied Saxon, Webster believed that he was in a position to correct the mistakes of Johnson and Lowth. He announced that he would not reprint his grammar until it was revised according to Tooke's principles. Johnson, according to Webster, had become the object of mindless veneration. Those who came after Johnson accepted his definitions without critically examining them. Half a century of dictionaries have thus falsely defined *misnomer, obligee, murder,* and *specially* among other words because of a slavish devotion to Johnson. In most cases Webster found the "correct" definitions of these words by tracing them back to their Saxon originals. His tendency to find the true meaning of a word in its radical was a habit that Webster would never lose.

While he maintained the notion that a knowledge of Saxon was essential for understanding English, other notions from the *Dissertations* had undergone considerable change. By 1806 he had given up all his radical ideas about spelling reform. The correct principle of orthography was moderation. A language could not tolerate drastic change, but "gradual changes to accommodate the written to the spoken language" were possible when they caused no inconvenience. Webster did suggest a list of "outlaws in orthography" where alterations might be made. He would reverse the concluding "re" in words such as *theatre* and *lustre* on the grounds that most English speakers pronounced the word *theater* and that the "re" form was clearly a corruption of French origin. Webster would also change the spelling of words that end in "que" or "quet." This change was authorized on the principle of analogy. Some words such as *masque* and *checquer* had been altered to *mask* and *checker* while *burlesque* and *pique* "retain their French livery." Webster opposed writing *defence, offence,* and *pretence;* he preferred "se" over "ce" because the derivatives of the words in question always used "se" (i.e., *defensive*). This was, by the way, one case in which he ignored the Saxon originals and employed another, more pragmatic principle. A fourth "outlaw" was the *u* in words like *honour* and *errour.* This alteration was sanctioned by two principles; in the derivatives the *u* was usually dropped and *honor* and its mates were simple Latin words corrupted by Norman French. Finally, Webster would drop the final *e* in *determine, discipline, examine,* and other like words because it was also a French corruption of good English.[9]

The publication of the *Compendious Dictionary* also marked several subtle changes in Webster's thought about pronunciation. Again, however, as in the *Dissertations* there were slight but significant contradictions. At one point, Webster stated that he held little hope for the establishment of a uniform pronunciation because "a living language admits of no fixed state, nor of any certain standard of pronunciation by which even the learned in general will consent to be governed." This plasticity did not stop him from proposing a standard, however. Rules for proper pronunciation should be based on *"the ease of pronunciation* and *melody of sounds."* Webster clearly thought these were organic principles, far superior to artificial ones that placed too much emphasis on rules taken from Latin and Greek. Later, he cited yet another rule to guide pronunciation. Surprisingly, he quoted Samuel Johnson's maxim "that those are the most elegant speakers, who deviate least from the written language." This rule, Webster contended, would erect a barrier "against the rage of innovation . . ." and was superior "to the authority of local usages. At this point, Webster revived, in slightly altered garb, a basic notion from the *Dissertations;* he asserted that Johnson's maxim was realized before the corruptions of Thomas Sheridan and John Walker in the eighteenth century. Thus we have the old notion that "true" and "pure" English was spoken in an earlier time, only to be unreasonably altered by "English authors who aim to fix a standard." Not surprisingly, this "true" spoken language was preserved in the speech of the "New England gentlemen" and the bulk of the English speakers who heroically fought off Sheridan and Walker's attempt to force them to speak the artificial "London dialect" that most scholars "considered a corruption." Thus, New England pronunciation met Johnson's standard and "is established on the authority of a thousand years practice . . ." (x–xi, xv–xvi).

Webster tried to remain faithful to an organic theory about the nature of change in pronunciation. He stated that "real improvements" arise from a popular tendency to abridge words which are difficult to pronounce, to soften or reject harsh letters and syllables, and to give to letters and syllables such sounds . . . as best suit the organs of utterance and of hearing." Yet this theory left Webster afraid that changes would arise from "the gay and fashionable world" and from people's tendency to imitate that "world." To avoid such capriciousness, Webster suggested to his readers that there was "a higher tribunal; the great body of literary and well-informed men in a nation, whose opinion of propriety is not to be seduced, nor their judgement perverted by the influence of names and fashion" (xvi). This elitism surely indicated a link between Webster's political and linguistic writings; the establishment of an elite to whom the people should pay deference was a part of both.

Earlier dictionaries had not only helped establish corrupt pronunciations, but they had also presented false etymologies of many words. Johnson was the major culprit; plagued by "his natural indolence, which led him to write often without investigation," and "disease and poverty," he wrote a "very imperfect" dictionary, "especially in the etymologies." Again Webster's reliance on Horne Tooke and his belief that Saxon was the key to understanding English led him to criticize an earlier writer. Johnson, for example, traced the English *obey* to the French *obéir*. To Webster, this was a howler, since the root was obviously the Saxon *abugan* from *began,* meaning *to bend.* The preface to the *Compendious Dictionary* was replete with such examples by which Webster used his new tool, the Saxon language, to undermine earlier authorities (xix).

The word list and definitions were hardly original. Webster admitted in the preface that his work was "an enlargement and improvement of Entick's spelling dictionary . . ." to which he claimed to have added nearly five thousand words. In general, the definitions seem short and vague to a modern reader. The spelling of controversial words generally followed standard method with the exception of the five "outlaws" he had noted in the preface. Following the definitions, he included an ample number of tables—the monetary systems of other countries, weights and measures, federal post offices, and the exports of each state. There was also a chronology of European history "from Creation to 1805" in which we discover that the world and Adam and Eve were created in 4004 B.C. (Cain was born a year later.)

Only rarely did Webster's political beliefs influence the dictionary. A "Federalist" was defined as "a friend of the Constitution of the United States," but the "Jeffersonians" or "Democrats" were nowhere to be found. A "Jacobin" lost his French historical reality and was generalized into a "member of a private club to overturn or manage government, one who opposes government in secret or unlawful manner or from an unreasonable spirit of discontent." In the chronology of American history George Washington was elected president but there was no mention of any others. The entry for 1800 included a great snow in the South, a "remarkable flood" in Connecticut, and the death of Washington.

The *Compendious Dictionary* was doubtless a learning experience for Webster. He discovered that American schools wanted a cheaper and smaller dictionary and he quickly turned out the *Dictionary of Schools* in 1807. This work was similar to the *Compendious Dictionary* but about one hundred pages shorter and printed in a smaller format. By 1807 Webster had gotten his feet wet as a maker of dictionaries; he was becoming familiar with the problems and processes associated with dictionaries. The products of 1806 and 1807 touched on themes that he would explore and expand for the next twenty years.[10]

An American Dictionary of the English Language

Webster completed *An American Dictionary* in January 1825 in Cambridge, England. Three years passed before it was published in New York—two quarto volumes, twenty dollars the set, 2,500 the first printing.[11] It was the heart of Webster's life; neither the schoolbooks, the newspapers, nor the political writings had required the devotion needed to make the dictionary. We know Webster, perhaps as well as any name from the early republic, because he wrote a dictionary. For the most part, the nature of the volume he published in 1828 has been lost. Some scholars have confused the Webster of 1828 with the Webster of 1785 and labeled the dictionary a nationalistic tract. Publishers, however, quietly eliminated Webster's philosophy of language from the work while retaining his name and some of his definitions. *An American Dictionary* revealed to some extent what Webster had become over a long life (he was seventy when it was first published). Nationalism and politics had long before taken a back seat to a profoundly religious consciousness.

The religious tone of the work was set by the dedication. *An American Dictionary* was dedicated to Webster's Christian God—"that great and benevolent being" who "sustained a feeble constitution." Webster made it clear that he was a servant to God and hoped that "if the talent which he entrusted to my care has not been put to the most profitable use in his service . . . it may be graciously forgiven." The religiosity extended to Webster's theory concerning the origin of language. For him language had supernatural roots. The Bible stated that Adam and Eve replied to God when they asked for forgiveness for their sin, and on this evidence he concluded that language, or at least speech, was "of divine origin" and that "all languages having sprung from one source, the original words from which they have been formed, must have been of equal antiquity."

For Webster, the multiplicity of languages on earth was also clearly explained in the Bible. The biblical Noah preserved not only animal life from the great flood, but language as well, and that language was Chaldee. Noah's sons settled on the plain of Shinar and spoke Chaldee until God, angered by the tower of Babel, "interposed and confounded their language, so they could not understand each other. . . ." The languages that resulted from this dispersion, Webster concluded, were equally ancient. He no longer resorted only to Saxon for root words but turned to what he considered man's most basic language—Chaldee or Chaldaic. Webster spent a decade creating a synopsis of the basic words in twenty languages, but too often his religious leanings pushed him to find at the beginning of a word's history an ancient Chaldee root. In this process he paid too little attention to vowels, which he came to see as meaningless, too much attention to consonants, and not enough to the similarity in sound between words that contain radically different letters.

Perhaps one of the best examples of what Webster produced using this method was his definition of *God*. His purpose was not solely to trace the history of a word through its transformations but also to discover its original meaning. Because the Saxon word for God was the same as the word for goodness, many people thought that, as Webster put it "God was named for his *goodness*." Webster disagreed; he traced the conception of God (mistaking it for the word) back to what he concluded it really meant: "I have found the name of the Supreme Being to be usually taken from his supremacy or power, and to be equivalent to lord or ruler, from some root signifying to press or exert force. Now in the present case, we have evidence that this is the sense of this word, for in Persic goda is rendered '*dominus, possessor, princeps.* . . .' "

It could hardly have been accidental that Webster's 1828 etymology of the word *God* reflected the transformation in his own religious sentiments. He had once seen God as love but after 1808 God became for him a much more malevolent and judgmental diety "equivalent to lord or ruler. . . ." In essence, Webster ignored the phonological truth that connected words in different languages and, instead, sought an elusive spiritual truth at the end of an etymological trail. He seemed to believe "that the truth of a word, that is the primitive and original radical value of a word, was equivalent to the truth of the idea. This is . . . the literal and original meaning of the word etymology, but not at all the sense which attaches to that word in the science of linguistics."[12]

Webster's etymological work was tarnished, in addition, by his isolation and provincialism. Although language study by 1820 had made great strides in Europe, Webster either dismissed European discoveries as misguided or was ignorant of them. For example, he dismissed the opinions of the English orientalist and jurist Sir William Jones who, based on his study of Sanskrit, believed Greek, Latin, and Sanskrit were derived from a common source (Indo-European) that no longer existed. Webster was ignorant of the scholars in the field who took up Jones's original suggestion. It seems inexcusable that Webster knew nothing of the work of Franz Bopp, who founded the new science of comparative grammar in 1816. Indeed, in the late eighteenth and early nineteenth centuries scholars were busy exploring the similarities observable in most of the known languages of Europe. They were able to group them into a family called Indo-European (the term first appeared in English in 1813). Webster, even though he traveled to Europe, remained blithely oblivious of these developments, clinging tenaciously to his own Bible-based theories. Yet his conclusions were remarkably similar in general outline to those of Jones and the others. The idea that all languages had one common ancestor was a basic conclusion of both Webster and Jones. One came to his findings by studying the Bible, while the others studied Sanskrit and its relation to Greek and Latin.

Even given this similarity, it does not explain Webster's woeful lack of knowledge of European linguistic scholarship. In part, his ignorance can be explained on the grounds that he had conditioned himself to ignore *European* authorities. He had spent his life asking Americans to turn away from a slavish dependence on Europe; perhaps by 1828 he had developed the habit of rejecting European scholarship out of hand. More important, however, was his religious temper. After his conversion, Webster grew more and more content to accept the Bible as the source of all truth. Such a temperament led easily to self-assurance and a tendency to avoid information that upset that self-assurance. Finally, he was a victim of America's general cultural isolation in the early years of the nineteenth century. By 1850 Americans were studying in Europe and bringing back the new scholarship in language studies. Webster wrote before this process began.

Provincialism of another sort found its way into the dictionary. Entitled *The American Dictionary*, it had, however, a decided New England flavor. Under his definition of *sauce* Webster informed his readers that "In New England, culinary vegetables and roots eaten with flesh" was an allowable definition of the word. Furthermore, the reader received the following advice: "*Sauce* consisting of stewed apples, is a great article in New England; but cranberries make the most delicious sauce." Bits of New England lore crop up in many places in the dictionary. For example, under *carpenter*, Webster passed along the New England distinction between a man who framed the house and the one who completed the interior work. It is very hard to conclude that a dictionary full of New England provincialisms was a nationalistic tract; Webster too often confused New England with the nation.

While it was marred by faulty etymological theories, provincialism, and a single-mindedness that deprived Webster of many advances in the study of language, *An American Dictionary* was still an amazing achievement. Before 1828 the largest available dictionaries listed between thirty-eight and fifty-eight thousand words. Webster's dictionary contained nearly seventy thousand. The additional listings included the participles of verbs, new common words, legal and scientific terms. Today a dictionary is compiled by a panel of experts each defining words in an area of human knowledge. Webster did it alone, and his forays into science, his legal training, and his boundless curiosity about nearly everything served him well.

The heart of any dictionary is, of course, its definitions. Webster made great improvements in this area over the dictionaries that then existed. Johnson's definitions, written in the middle of the eighteenth century, were clearly antiques by 1825. For example, Johnson had defined *mortgage* as "A dead pledge; a thing put into the hands of a creditor." Webster noted that it meant that literally, but goes on to define the word as "the grant of an estate in fee as security for the payment of money, and on the condition that if the amount shall be paid according to the contract, the grant shall be void, and mortgages shall reconvey the estate to the mortgager." In general, Webster's definitions were more complete and modern than Johnson's and those who had often blindly copied him. There can be no doubt that Webster's dictionary was more useful to the Americans who purchased it than any other available to them at the time.

The definitions and the examples of usage supplied by Webster, however, revealed his political and religious preferences. *An American Dictionary* was written by a conservative Christian man. Under the verb form of *love,* for example, Webster included the following examples of usage: "The Christian *loves* his Bible. In short, we *love* whatever gives us pleasure and delight . . . and if our hearts are right, we *love* God above all things, as the sum of all excellence and all the attributes which can communicate happiness to intelligent beings." The definition of *duty* also reflected Webster's conservative Christian leanings; he defined *duty* as

That which a person owes to another; that which a person is bound, by any natural, moral or legal obligation, to pay, do or perform. Obedience to princes, magistrates and the laws is the *duty* of every citizen and subject; obedience, respect and kindness to parents are the *duties* of children; fidelity to friends is a *duty;* reverence, obedience and prayer to God are indisputable *duties;* the government and religious instruction of children are *duties* of parents which they cannot neglect without guilt.

Clearly Webster used the dictionary to express his feelings on a number of matters. We can only guess what went through his mind when, for example, he came to write the entry for *education:*

The bringing up, as of a child; instruction; formation of manners. Education comprehends all that series of instruction and discipline which is intended to enlighten the understanding, correct the temper, and form the manners and habits of youth, and fit them for usefulness in their future stations. To give children a good education in manners, arts and sciences, is important, to give them a religious education is indispensable; an immense responsibility rests on parents and guardians who neglect these duties.

In these few lines he summarized fifty years of thought on education. Most Americans who read this definition would have found little to quibble with.

Americans in the 1830s also would have found little fault with his definition of *sex* as "the distinction between male and female. . . . The male sex is usually characterized by muscular strength, boldness and firmness. The female sex is characterized by softness, sensibility and modesty." Nor would they have debated his choice of examples of usage for the word *woman:* "*Women* are soft, mild, pitiful, and flexible" and "We see everyday *women* perish with infamy, by having been too willing to set their beauty to show." Americans generally nodded agreement to Webster's sample of usage under the word *employ:* "A portion of time should be *employed* in reading the Scriptures, meditation and prayer; a great portion of life is *employed* to little profit or to very bad purposes."

The definitions in *An American Dictionary* reflected a conservative, Christian society that wanted to control their children and train them for useful occupations. The same society viewed women as weaker and inferior to men; Americans generally were also imbued with the values of thrift and responsibility to authority. There existed, of course, segments of American culture that, no doubt, would have found fault with Webster's definitions, but the dominant culture and especially those crucial arbiters of such works as dictionaries—the churches, the colleges, and literary reviews—found Webster's dictionary acceptable. Webster certainly grew anachronistic in his old age, but he never entirely lost contact with his culture. Indeed, by becoming the most widely accepted authority on the meaning of words, Webster helped establish conservative and Christian values as dominant in his culture.

A spirit of moderation marked many aspects of *An American Dictionary*, and this, no doubt, helped it become an accepted standard reference. When the spelling of a word was contested, Webster "aimed at consistency and uniformity" and "followed the decided tendency of the public mind, both in this country and England." Webster still produced some radical suggestions; for example, he proposed *bridegoom* for *bridegroom* because the former was the spelling of the Saxon original, the latter being a corruption. For similar reasons he changed *build* to *bild* and *island* to *ieland*. These examples illustrated the continued influence that his etymological research had on his opinions. He often found in the original Saxon spelling a compelling argument for changing contemporary orthography that was sanctioned by centuries of use. The suggested spelling changes, however, were relatively few in a dictionary of seventy thousand words, and, in many cases, Webster silently dropped his earlier reformed spellings and retained reformed spellings as a second choice as in *lether* and *fether* for *leather* and *feather*. In other instances, he simply followed conventional ways by changing the 1806 spelling of *bason* to *basin*, *letice* to *lettuce*, and the final *e* was restored to *definite*, *doctrine*, *examine*, and the like. Webster never totally gave up his desire to reform spelling but by 1828 the desire to appear conventional was successfully combating the desire to change and purify.

Webster's moderation was also evident in a lessening of his hostility toward England and his demand for a distinctively American language. He still believed that Americans should have their own dictionary, but it was good to perpetuate "a sameness" between American and British English. The differences that do exist, Webster suggested, were largely a matter of differences in government, legal system, and social customs. He argued that since the United States had no royalty or feudal tradition, there would have to be a corresponding difference in language. Each nation would need to use words that fit its own political and social structure. As for so-called "Americanisms," he thought there were not very many. Words that people considered distinctively American were simply modified versions of words used for centuries in England. Webster's patriotism was most clearly evident in his use of American authors to illustrate the usage of words. He believed that Washington and Franklin "present as pure models of genuine English as Addison and Swift." This flash of patriotism was a considerably subdued version of the zeal that Webster exhibited in the 1780s. It also reflected his political leanings by including many Federalists and ignoring others, such as Jefferson.

Even though Webster modified many of his views, it did not exempt him from criticism. In 1831 Lyman Cobb published *A Critical Review of the Orthography of Dr. Webster's Series of Books for Systematick Instruction in the English Language*. Cobb's intentions were only partially those of a scholar; he had written a spelling book that he hoped would capture some of Webster's huge audience and it eventually did. To a large extent, the conflict centered around spelling, with Cobb using Walker's dictionary as a standard to measure the modest reforms proposed by Webster. With some justice, he also charged Webster with inconsistency. The two men hurled charges at each other, often with the aim of reducing the prestige of the other in the minds of those who purchased schoolbooks. Cobb granted Webster his achievement but insisted that the schools needed new books: Webster's "zeal for something different from English has led him to adopt innovations without regard to their defects, propriety, consistency, or uniformity . . . he has adopted an easier method, that of condemning every English lexicographer . . . who has been so presumptuous and unfortunate as to disagree with his favorite notions of innovations in orthography."[13] In retrospect all this seemed like a puffed-up debate over a small matter in which no one emerged covered with glory. It illustrated that *An American Dictionary* was often received by Webster's critics in the context of his earlier work. He had been pigeonholed as a rabid Americanist who sought to undermine the standards established by Johnson, Sheridan, and Walker, and his 1828 dictionary was received in this way by many critics.

Such charges were clearly misguided. The innovations proposed by Webster in 1828 were small and his reverence for British authorities large. He could not abide Walker's suggested pronunciations and stated his reasons clearly. As for the great Samuel Johnson, he referred to him as "one of the greatest men that the English nation has ever produced." By 1828, because of earlier criticism or as a natural outgrowth of his increasing conservatism, Webster was far from an innovator. Regarding pronunciation, for example, he demanded uniformity and regularity, harshly condemning "the fashion of the day" as a guide for proper speech. His test of proper pronunciation was "the usage of respectable people in England and the United States," and when this test did not provide a suitable pronunciation, he fell back on analogies to similar words with some regard for "melody." *An American Dictionary* assumed that American and British English were overwhelmingly the same. On both sides of the Atlantic, English was "a nervous, masculine language, well adapted to popular eloquence. . . ." There may be, Webster thought, "some connection between this manly character of the language and the freedom of the British and American constitutions."

The debate over the dictionary did not die with Webster. The history of Webster's dictionary is long and complex and full of controversy. A second edition came out in 1841, and after Webster's death in 1843 George and Charles Merriam purchased the unsold stock of the second edition and soon its sale and promotion became their sole business. The brothers hired Chauncy A. Goodrich, Webster's son-in-law, to edit a new edition. This inexpensive (six dollars), one-volume version took hold and probably did more to make Webster's name synonymous with dictionary than any other factor. Noah Porter edited the unabridged edition in 1864, and editions and versions regularly appeared until 1934 when Webster's work was completely rewritten and revised in the so-called *Second Edition*. Between 1828 and 1934, however, much of Webster's thought was quietly removed from the work; in 1864 the etymologies from 1828 disappeared and were replaced by those constructed by C. A. F. Mahn. This edition is often called the Webster-Mahn dictionary.

As Webster's 1828 masterwork was being transformed by other hands into a modern dictionary, a war broke out—the so-called War of the Dictionaries. Across the battlefield from Webster's dictionary stood the unlikely figure of Joseph Emerson Worcester (1784–1865). The product of a New Hampshire farm and Yale, Worcester spent the early part of his life as a geographer and editor. In 1830 he wrote a small dictionary and devoted the rest of his life to enlarging and improving it. In 1860 he published *A Dictionary of the English Language;* a huge 1,786-page work, it contested for some years against *An American Dictionary* for first place in the hearts of Americans. The battle was fired by the passions of salesmen who sought to sell either Webster or Worcester to schools and states. In the mid-nineteenth century state legislatures often adopted a dictionary by legislative act for public and school use and such adoptions meant thousands of dol-

lars to publishers. Several modern critics have concluded that
Worcester's dictionary was generally superior to Webster's but that
Webster won the war through superior editing, merchandising, and
salesmanship.[14]

Any final analysis of Webster's dictionary must ignore the pleas
and distortions of salesmen, but then how does one judge a dictionary? In the first place, *An American Dictionary* was a crucial, culmi-
nating document in Noah Webster's life. It reflected the fact that religious sentiment had risen to a central place in his life. The political
pamphleteer, the enlightened scientist, and the embattled editor had
vanished in favor of a scholar who saw himself as God's obedient servant. His acceptance of and reliance on biblical literalism in the introduction to his Dictionary would have been impossible in 1787. Furthermore, in the context of the time it was an extraordinary piece of
work. Written by one man, with limited resources, *An American Dictionary* was a landmark in American culture. Along with Emerson's
American Scholar, Webster's dictionary helped to establish the United
States as more than a political experiment in republicanism; it dem-
onstrated that the New World would produce more than frontier leg-
ends and political parties. Webster's cultural nationalism was often
more than a little disingenuous; it was often self-serving and provincial but the works he produced, especially the dictionary, went a long
way toward making the United States a credible influence in the
world of culture and scholarship.

The dictionary was only the culmination of Webster's lifelong devotion to language. He spent his life manipulating words for a number of purposes. Always the taciturn Yankee, he never engaged in
much self-analysis and never revealed why he felt that he had turned
to words as the major passion of his life. Yet, in a way, the reason is
fairly clear; from 1783 to 1843 he was also intensely interested in the
problem of authority. Those sixty years witnessed dramatic shifts in
the way Americans and the world conceived and structured authority.
A significant aspect of the transformation in authority relationships
was a corresponding shift in language. In 1783 *democracy* was a term
of derision for many, the word *demoralized* had not yet been invented,
and the English language was only beginning to rise to its place as
the principal language in the West. By 1843 much of this had
changed; politics, morals, and language were transformed as man re-
thought the nature of authority. Webster believed that authority had
to rest on absolute principles and that those principles must, by the

nature of man, be expressed in language. To control and direct the opinions of men one could employ force, or better, one could control language. Thus, Webster, anxious about the rapid disintegration of authority he thought he saw all around him, sought to ascertain the primal meanings of words so that men could know the truth. His desire to find the "primary signification" of words was, in the final analysis, motivated by his need to arrest the swirling transformations of a revolutionary age.

Chapter Six

Epilogue

In 1833, at age seventy-five, Noah Webster published a work that he called "the most important enterprise of my life. . . ." It was his own version of the King James Bible. The language and grammar of the King James version had long offended Webster; his New England prudery objected to some of the words, so he changed "to give suck" to "to nourish," "to go a-whoring" to "to go astray," and "teat" to "breast." He transformed obscure words into more modern language so that the Bible would be more understandable. Thus, *let* became *hinder, sodden* became *boiled* and *kine* became *cows.* He believed that children learned faulty grammar from the Bible, so he substituted *who* for *which,* changed present subjunctives into future indicatives, and tinkered with mismatched subjects and verbs. In the end, he produced the last link in his system of education for Americans—a speller, a grammar, a reader, a dictionary, and finally a Bible.

The publication of his version of the Bible was the end of Webster's quest to provide his fellow citizens with new, sound sources of authority. Before the American Revolution was over, a young Noah Webster had been busy seeking a new basis upon which to base American lives. He spent the balance of his life explaining, cajoling, and debating with the American people. Even before his religious conversion, he sounded very much like a New England minister instructing his congregation on their duties and responsibilities. In his quest for new sources of authority he was rarely, if ever, philosophical; Webster tended to reject the metaphysical treatise aimed at the few. Instead, he wrote simple and practical books for the common people. He gave them a spelling book that urged Americans to have pride in the differences between New and Old World English. Americans should cast off their dependence on British authorities and rely on a rising American elite that Webster wanted desperately to join. The spelling book was also a lesson in virtue; it taught the simple values of thrift, piety, and common sense.

A central part of Webster's lifelong crusade for stable authority was political. He urged the people to put political power in the hands of a virtuous and learned elite who understood the principles of justice and the common good. Like many of his New England contemporaries, he never fully accepted the direct and constant participation of the people in political affairs. The federal Constitution embodied many of Webster's deepest wishes for the American government. It would, he hoped, check the voice of the people, liberate the legislature from the constant demands of a discontented people, and provide the executive power capable of vigorously enforcing the laws. During his tenure as editor and owner of the *Minerva* Webster wrote volumes in an attempt to reconcile the people to their new constitutional government, but by 1800 he had begun to despair. The new frame of government did not check the political passions of the people; they would not let duly constituted authority run the nation unmolested. Appalled by the rise of factions, the bitter contest between Democrats and Federalists and partisan journalism, Webster retreated from New York to his beloved New England. Spiritually, he never left again.

During the very last years of the eighteenth century Webster began to realize that schools, schoolbooks, and a federal Constitution would not create a stable and orderly republic. Authority must rest on some unshakable bedrock. His New England heritage provided that bedrock—the God of John Calvin modified and redefined for nineteenth-century use. The quest for authority came to a climax when Webster found God and the idea of submission to the laws of the Bible. His whole life changed dramatically after his conversion in 1808. Even his dictionaries and language theory reflected his newfound devotion to God. The dictionary that he published in 1828 was written by the light of the Bible. Speech became the gift of God to man and the meaning of words had to conform to his new religious sentiments. Everywhere in his thought after 1800 one finds submission, subordination, and order as the dominant ideas. Oddly, he persisted in his demands for reform and change. Much like the radical abolitionists, Webster called for Americans to repent and change their ways. The feeling that Americans must reject natural liberty and riotous independence for the sake of some higher good was the cord that tied his life together.

His quest for authority was the product of two conflicts—one intellectual and one social. Webster lived during an era when Enlightenment ideas and Protestant thought clashed fundamentally. Much of the Enlightenment survived, but as Henry May has concluded, in order to survive, enlightened ideas "had to be accommodated to the

other and older source of American culture: Christianity in its myriad
and shifting American forms."[1] Calvinism became the form of Christianity that did battle with the Enlightenment in Webster's mind.
He never, however, became a stereotypical product of either influence; submission to God and a belief in progress resided uncomfort-
ably together in his mind. While the conflict between enlightened
ideas and Christianity was disrupting the lines of authority, socially
America was beginning to experience a conflict between the social
realities of rural life and a growing cosmopolitanism. Webster felt the
influence of both. Raised in the rural Connecticut countryside, he
lived and worked much of his life in American cities. The values of
his childhood conflicted with the sophistication of New York and
Philadelphia. The pull of the New England farm and its values
proved strong indeed; Webster never lost his faith in them. These
two conflicts, more than any others, disrupted the stability of America. Webster was only one of many Americans, caught in that disrup-
tion, who sought to rise above it and find a new order.

Any historical event, and certainly any life, is only partially re-
trievable. Noah Webster will always remain a puzzle for us. His early
life is largely lost so we shall never know for sure what forces drove
him to books and study and away from the farm. We shall never
know enough about the relationship between the young Noah and his
father. We shall never know for sure the source of his despair and
depression in the early 1780s. We can only guess at the forces that
drove him to work himself to the verge of mental and physical col-
lapse. Yet he remains an important figure for those who would make
sense out of post-revolutionary American life. While he was never a
great political theorist, poet, or artist, Webster labored in an extraordinary number of fields: politics, language, science, journalism, and
education. Because of this he stands as a barometer revealing the pressures and anxieties felt by all Americans confronting a changing
world. His massive body of writings is the record of a man who began his adult life full of utopian dreams for America and whose last
years were full of gloom because he thought one of mankind's most
crucial experiments was going to fail.

Notes and References

Chapter One

1. This chapter is based in large part on Richard M. Rollins, *The Long Journey of Noah Webster* (Philadelphia, 1980); Harry R. Warfel, *Noah Webster: Schoolmaster to America* (New York, 1936); Joseph J. Ellis, *After the Revolution: Profiles of Early American Culture* (New York, 1979).

2. 20 December 1808, Harry R. Warfel, *Letters of Noah Webster* (New York, 1953), p. 309; hereafter cited as *Letters*.

3. Rollins, *Long Journey*, pp. 9–12.

4. Ervin C. Shoemaker, *Noah Webster: Pioneer of Learning* (New York, 1936), p. 20.

5. As quoted in ibid., p. 15.

6. As quoted in Warfel, *Schoolmaster to America*, p. 29.

7. As quoted in Shoemaker, *Pioneer of Learning*, p. 17.

8. Rollins, *Long Journey*, p. 19.

9. Ibid., pp. 21–22.

10. 18 January 1783, *Letters*, pp. 5–7.

11. 24 October 1782, ibid.

12. 19 January 1785 and 15 February 1785, ibid., pp. 19–31.

13. 20 January 1786, ibid., pp. 43–44.

14. Emily E. F. Ford, compiler, *Notes on the Life of Noah Webster* 2 vols. (New York: [privately printed], 1912), vol. I, p. 46.

15. 18 December 1785, *Letters*, p. 43.

16. 25 April 1787, ibid., p. 60.

17. 20 June 1787, 11 October 1788, and 27 January 1788, ibid., pp. 69–73.

18. Rollins, *Long Journey*, pp. 76–78.

19. 6 July 1798, *Letters*, pp. 181–82.

20. 15 December 1800, Ford, *Notes*, vol. I, p. 479.

21. 22 January 1802, ibid., p. 524.

22. 2 March 1801, *Letters*, p. 230.

23. 20 December 1808, ibid., p. 310.

24. 16 December 1782, Ford, *Notes*, vol. I, p. 56.

25. Ibid., pp. 312–13.

26. Quoted in Henry May, *The Enlightenment in America* (New York, 1976), p. 319.

27. The Great Revival has been the subject of a number of studies. Perhaps most useful are C. R. Keller, *The Second Great Awakening in Connecticut* (New Haven: Yale University Press, 1924), Perry Miller, "From the Cove-

nant to the Revival," in J. W. Smith and A. L. Jamison, eds., *The Shaping of American Religion* (Princeton, N.J.: Princeton University Press, 1961), D. G. Mattews, "The Second Great Awakening as an Organizing Process, 1780–1830: An Hypothesis," *American Quarterly* (Spring 1969), and Richard D. Birdsall, "The Second Great Awakening and the New England Social Order," *Church History* (1970).

28. *Hampshire Gazette,* 3 December 1817.
29. 6 September 1834, *Letters,* p. 444.
30. Quoted in Warfel, *Schoolmaster to America,* p. 55.
31. Ford, *Notes,* vol. I, p. 293.
32. Quoted in Warfel, *Schoolmaster to America,* p. 423.
33. 3 July 1840, quoted in Rollins, *Long Journey,* p. 141.
34. Ibid., p. 140.

Chapter Two

1. The best source for the publishing history of Webster's many works is Edwin H. Carpenter, ed., *A Bibliography of the Writings of Noah Webster* (New York, 1958).
2. A. M. Colton, "Our Old Webster Spelling Book," *Magazine of American History* 24 (1890): 467.
3. *Noah Webster's Spelling Book* (1831 edition), with an introduction by Henry Steele Commager (New York, 1962), p. 38.
4. Quoted in Shoemaker, *Pioneer,* p. 91.
5. *Noah Webster's Spelling Book,* p. 163.
6. Quoted in Shoemaker, *Pioneer,* p. 73.
7. *The American Spelling Book: Containing an Easy Standard of Pronunciation . . .* (Hartford: 1793), p. x.
8. 6 January 1783, *Letters,* p. 4.
9. Ibid.
10. *A Grammatical Institute . . .* Part II (Hartford: 1784), p. iv.
11. Ibid., (1787 edition), p. v.
12. *An American Selection . . .* (Philadelphia: 1787), p. 16; hereafter cited in text as *AS.*
13. *History of the United States . . .* (New Haven, 1832), p. 6; hereafter cited in text as *H.*
14. 24 July 1832, *Letters,* p. 431.
15. "On the Education of Youth in America," reprinted in Frederick Rudolph, ed., *Essays on Education in the Early Republic* (Cambridge, Mass.: Harvard University Press, 1965); hereafter cited in text as *ED.*
16. "Letter to a Young Gentleman Commencing his Education," in Noah Webster, *A Collection of Papers on Political, Literary and Moral Subjects* (1843), p. 295; hereafter cited in text as *Co.*

17. Lawrence Cremin, *Traditions of American Education* (New York, 1977), pp. 85–86.

18. 30 October 1837 and 27 February 1841, *Letters,* pp. 507, 518.

19. 30 March, 1820, ibid., p. 400.

20. 30 October 1837, ibid., p. 507.

Chapter Three

1. May 1843?, *Letters,* p. 525.

2. *Freeman's Chronicle,* 10 November 1783.

3. *New York Packet,* 31 January 1782.

4. *Freeman's Chronicle,* 10 November 1783.

5. Ibid., 20 October 1783.

6. *Sketches of American Policy* (New York: Scholars Facsimiles and Reprints, 1937). Edited with introduction by Harry R. Warfel, pp. 6–10; hereafter cited in text as *Sk.*

7. These notes are in Webster's copy of *Sketches* in the New York Public Library. The remark from the letter to Morse is quoted in Carpenter, *Bibliography,* p. 306. Carpenter also includes a good selection of Webster's marginal notes in the *Sketches.*

8. *An Examination into the Leading Principles of the Federal Constitution* . . . (Philadelphia, 1787), pp. 6–8; hereafter page references cited in parentheses in the text.

9. "Government," *American Magazine* (1787–1788), pp. 75, 142; hereafter page references cited in parentheses in the text.

10. (Hartford) *Connecticut Courant,* 12 August 1783. Quoted in Gordon Wood, *The Creation of the American Republic 1776–1787* (New York, 1969), p. 382. My discussion of the Giles Hickory essays owes a heavy debt to Wood's analysis. His work is the best available discussion of political thought between the Revolution and the Constitution.

11. "Revolution in France," in *A Collection of Papers on Political, Literary and Moral Subjects* (New York: 1843), p. 3; cited in text as *Co.*

12. *An Oration, Pronounced before the Citizens of New Haven . . . July 4th, 1798* (New Haven: 1798) and *An Oration, Pronounced before the Citizens of New Haven, on the Anniversary of the Declaration of Independence . . .* (New Haven: 1802); hereafter cited in text by year, followed by page number.

13. October 1800, *Letters,* p. 244.

14. Ibid., p. 242.

15. Ibid., Letters I and X, pp. 206–7, 215.

16. Ibid., Letter III, pp. 208–9.

17. Ibid., Letter I, pp. 204–5.

18. Ibid., Letters IX and X, pp. 210–14.

19. Ibid., Letter X, p. 214.

20. Ibid., New Haven, 1837, p. 497. Signed "Marcellus."
21. Ibid., 29 August 1837, p. 505. Signed "Sidney."
22. Ibid., New Haven, 1837, p. 493.
23. Ibid., p. 488–89.
24. Ibid., 1837?, p. 513.

Chapter Four

1. Introduction, to *American Magazine* (December 1787), p. 4.
2. See particularly 9 February 1788, *Letters,* pp. 74–76.
3. *The Prompter* . . . (Boston, 1794), p. 5; hereafter cited in text as *Pr,* followed by year and page number.
4. *American Minerva,* 1 May 1796.
5. Ibid., 5 August 1795, also, 18 July 1795.
6. Ibid., 1 May 1796.
7. Ford, *Notes,* vol. I, p. 380.

Chapter Five

1. *Dissertations of the English Language: With Notes Historical and Critical* . . . (Boston: 1789), p. ix; hereafter page references cited in parentheses in the text.
2. Quoted in George Philip Krapp, *The English Language in America* (New York, 1925), p. 330.
3. *A Collection of Essays and Fugitiv Writings* . . . (Boston: 1790), pp. x–xi.
4. Krapp, *The English Language,* p. 334.
5. This essay is most readily available reprinted in Noah Webster, *A Collection* . . . , 1790, cited above, pp. 222–28.
6. The announcement is quoted at length in Warfel, *Schoolmaster to America,* p. 289.
7. The criticisms of Webster are quoted from ibid., pp. 291–94; see also *Letters,* p. 247, for a sample of Webster's response.
8. Krapp, *The English Language,* pp. 358–59.
9. *A Compendious Dictionary of the English Language* (New Haven: 1806), pp. viii–ix; hereafter page references cited in parentheses in the text.
10. See, for example, Webster's letter to John Jay, 19 May 1813, in *Letters,* pp. 334–35.
11. *An American Dictionary of the English Language* (New York: 1828). The front matter in this edition has no page numbers. All quotations, unless noted, in the remainder of this chapter are from that front matter or from the definitions in the body of the work.
12. Krapp, *The English Language,* pp. 364–65.
13. Quoted in Warfel, *Schoolmaster to America,* pp. 388–89.

14. Both Krapp, in *The English Language,* p. 372, and Charlton Laird in *Language in America* (Englewood Cliffs, N.J., 1970), pp. 287–88, suggest that Worcester's was the better dictionary.

Chapter Six

1. Henry F. May, *The Enlightenment in America* (New York, 1976), p. 361.

Selected Bibliography

PRIMARY SOURCES

1. Bibliography and compilations

Carpenter, Edwin H., ed. *A Bibliography of the Writings of Noah Webster.* New York: New York Public Library, 1958. The starting point for any study of Webster. Provides a list of Webster's works along with information about the many editions of each work, places rare editions can be found, and a great deal more.

Ford, Emily Ellsworth Fowler, comp., and Skeel, Emily Ellsworth Ford, ed. *Notes on the Life of Noah Webster.* 2 vols. New York: privately printed, 1912. Also a fundamental source of information on Webster. It contains letters to and from Webster, plus his diary along with a running commentary by the compiler and editor who are descendents of Webster.

Warfel, Harry R., ed. *Letters of Noah Webster.* New York: Library Publishers, 1953. Contains a good sample of Webster's personal correspondence and a few of his public letters which are hard to find elsewhere.

2. Works by Noah Webster

An American Dictionary of the English Language. New York: S. Converse, 1828.

――――. *An American selection of lessons in reading and speaking.* Philadelphia: Young and McCulloch, 1787.

――――. *The American Spelling Book, Being the FIRST PART of a GRAMMATICAL INSTITUTE of the English Language.* Boston: Thomas and Andrews, 1789.

――――. *A Brief History of Epidemic and Pestilential Diseases.* 2 vols. Hartford: Hudson and Goodwin, 1799.

――――. *A Collection of Essays and Fugitiv Writings on Moral, Historical, Political and Literary Subjects.* Boston: J. Thomas and E. T. Andrews, 1790.

――――. *A Collection of Papers on Political, Literary and Moral Subjects.* New York: Burt Franklin, Research and Source Works Series 249, 1843.

――――. *A Compendious Dictionary of the English Language.* New Haven: Hudson and Goodwin, 1806.

――――. *Dissertations on the English Language: With Notes, Historical and Critical.* Boston: Isaiah Thomas, 1789.

_____. *Effects of Slavery on Morals and Industry.* Hartford: Hudson and Goodwin, 1793.

_____. *An Examination into the leading principles of the federal constitution proposed by the late Convention held at Philadelphia. With answers to the principal objections that have been raised against the system. By a citizen of America.* Philadelphia: Pritchard and Hall, 1787.

_____. *A grammatical Institute of the English Language, comprising, an easy, concise, and systematic method of education, designed for the use of English schools in America. In three parts. Part I.* Hartford: Hudson and Goodwin, 1783.

_____. *A grammatical institute . . . Part II.* Hartford: Hudson and Goodwin, 1784.

_____. *A grammatical institute . . . Part III.* Hartford: Barlow and Babcock, 1785.

_____. *History of the United States; to which is prefixed a brief historical account of our English ancestors from the dispersion of Babel, to their migration to America.* New Haven: Durrie and Peck, 1832.

_____. *History of the United States.* Cincinnati: Cory, Fairbank and Webster, 1835.

_____. *The Holy Bible, containing the Old and New Testaments, in the common version. With amendments of the language.* New Haven: Durrie and Peck, 1833.

_____. *The Little Readers' Assistant.* Hartford: Elisha Babcock, 1790.

_____. *Miscellaneous Papers on Political and Commercial Subjects.* New York: Burt Franklin American Classics in History and Social Sciences Series 10, 1802.

_____. *Noah Webster's Spelling Book.* New York: Bureau of Publications, Teacher's College, Columbia University, 1962. This is a reprint of the 1831 edition of the spelling book with an introductory essay by Henry Steele Commager. It is the most readily available edition of the spelling book.

_____. *Observations on language, and on the errors of class-books; Also, observations on commerce.* New Haven: S. Babcock, 1839.

_____. *On Being American: Selected Writings 1783-1828.* New York: Praeger, 1967. Edited and introduction by Homer D. Babbidge, Jr.

_____. *An Oration, Pronounced before the Citizens of New Haven on the Anniversary of the Declaration of Independence of the United States, July 4th, 1798.* New Haven: T. and S. Green. 1798.

_____. *An Oration, Pronounced before the Citizens of New Haven, on the Anniversary of the Declaration of Independence: July, 1802.* New Haven: William W. Morse, 1802.

_____. *The Prompter; A Commentary on Common Sayings and Subjects, which are of Common Sense, the Best Sense in the World. A New Edition, improved and Enlarged.* New Haven: Joel Walter, 1803.

————. *The Prompter; or a Commentary on Common Sayings and Subjects.* . . . Boston: I. Thomas and E. T. Andrews, 1794.

————. *The Revolution in France considered in respect to its progress and effects. By an American.* New York: George Bunce, 1794.

————. *Sketches of American Policy.* 1785. Reprint. New York: Scholars Facsimiles and Reprints, 1937.

SECONDARY SOURCES

Bailyn, Bernard. *The Ideological Origins of the American Revolution.* Cambridge: Harvard University Press, 1967.

Banner, James M., Jr. *To the Hartford Convention: The Federalist and the Origins of Party Politics in Massachusetts, 1789-1815.* New York: Knopf, 1970.

Benton, Joel. "Unwritten Chapter in Noah Webster's Life: Love and the Spelling Book." *Magazine of American History* 10 (July 1883):52–56. An account of Webster's romantic failures early in life and their influence on his career.

Cremin, Lawrence A. *Traditions of American Education.* New York: Basic Books, 1977.

Ellis, Joseph J. *After the Revolution: Profiles of Early American Culture.* New York: W. W. Norton, 1979. This book contains the best short account of Webster's life and work along with a number of other commendable essays on figures who, like Webster, had to live in a post-revolutionary world.

————. "Habits of Mind and an American Enlightenment." *American Quarterly* 28 (1976):150–64. An essay that summarizes past work on the Enlightenment and suggests that paradox and tension are keys to understanding its impacts.

Elson, Ruth Miller. *Guardians of Tradition: American Schoolbooks of the Nineteenth Century.* Lincoln: University of Nebraska Press, 1964. An analysis of the values that dominated schoolbooks during Webster's time.

Friend, Joseph H. *The Development of American Lexicography, 1798-1864.* The Hague: Mouton, 1967. A technical analysis of early American dictionaries by a man who once worked on the Webster dictionary.

Johnson, Clifton. *Old Time Schools and School-Books.* New York: Dover, 1963.

Krapp, George P. *The English Language in America.* 2 vols. New York: Frederick Ungar, 1925. The best general account of the growth of the language in America. Contains balanced judgments on Webster's spelling book and dictionaries.

Laird, Charlton. *Language in America.* Englewood Cliffs, N.J.: Prentice-

Hall, 1970. A readable general account of language in America that has several good sections on Webster.

Leavitt, Robert. *Noah's Ark: New England Yankees and the Endless Quest.* Springfield, Mass.: Merriam, 1947. A celebrationist tract that emphasizes the dictionary.

Lewis, W. David. "The Reformers as Conservatives: Protestant Counter-Subversion in the Early Republic." In *The Development of an American Culture,* edited by Stanley Coben and Lorman Ratner. Englewood Cliffs, N.J.: Prentice-Hall, 1970. An excellent introduction to the problem of religious conservative thought in the early nineteenth century.

Mathews, Donald G. "The Second Great Awakening as an Organizing Process, 1780-1830: An Hypothesis." *American Quarterly* 21 (1969): 23–43. Suggests that social factors may have been more important than intellectual anxiety in causing the religious revival.

May, Henry. *The Enlightenment in America.* New York: Oxford University Press, 1976. A central work. The last third of the book is particularly central in understanding the context in which Webster lived.

Miller, John C. *The Federalist Era, 1789-1801.* New York: Harper and Row, 1960. A basic survey of the decade that changed Webster so much.

Morgan, John S. *Noah Webster.* New York: Mason-Charter, 1975. A good general biography of Webster that ignores many of the problems posed by Webster and attempts to present an objective portrait, but does not.

Mott, Frank Luther. *American Journalism: A History of Newspapers in the United States through 250 Years, 1690-1940.* New York: Macmillan, 1941. Basic starting point for exploring Webster's career as journalist.

Pyles, Thomas. *Words and Ways of American English.* New York: Random House, 1952. Has two interesting but general chapters on Webster. See particularly "Noah Webster, Man and Symbol."

Richardson, Lyon N. *A History of Early American Magazines, 1741-1789.* New York: Thomas Nelson, 1931. A good starting point for any study of early magazines. May have seen the *American Magazine* as better than it actually was.

Rollins, Richard M. *The Long Journey of Noah Webster.* Philadelphia: University of Pennsylvania Press, 1980. The most recent biography. Attempts to swing the focus away from Webster's nationalism and puts the stress on his conservatism in later life. Contains an excellent bibliography.

⸻. "Noah Webster: Propagandist for the Revolution." *Connecticut History* 18 (1976):22:43.

⸻. "Words as Social Control: Noah Webster and the Creation of the

American Dictionary." *American Quarterly* 28 (1976):415–30. Argues that religious sentiment was more influential than patriotism or nationalism in shaping the *American Dictionary*.

Scudder, Horace E. *Noah Webster.* Boston: Houghton Mifflin, 1883. The first biography of Webster. Scudder emphasized Webster's vanity and efforts at self-promotion.

Shoemaker, Ervin C. *Noah Webster: Pioneer of Learning.* New York: Columbia University Press, 1936. Exhaustive analysis of Webster's schoolbooks and his educational theory.

Smelser, Marshall. "The Federal Period as an Age of Passion." *American Quarterly* 10 (1958): 391–419.

Warfel, Harry R. *Noah Webster: Schoolmaster to America.* New York: Macmillan, 1936. The fullest biography of Webster available. Touches on all aspects of his life but tends to celebrate Webster rather than explain him.

Warthin, Aldred S. "Noah Webster as Epidemiologist." *Journal of American Medical Association* 80 (1923):755–64.

Winslow, Charles-Edward A. "The Epidemiology of Noah Webster." *Transactions of the Connecticut Academy of Arts and Sciences* 32 (1934):23–109.

Wood, Gordon. *Creation of the American Republic.* Chapel Hill: University of North Carolina Press, 1969.

Index